THE
STAVE CHURCH
PAINTINGS

THE STAVE CHURCH PAINTINGS

Mediaeval Art from Norway

INTRODUCTION BY

MARTIN BLINDHEIM

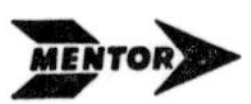

A MENTOR-UNESCO ART BOOK

PUBLISHED BY
THE NEW AMERICAN LIBRARY, INC.
BY ARRANGEMENT WITH UNESCO

FIRST PRINTING, DECEMBER, 1965

MENTOR TRADEMARK REG. U. S. PAT. OFF. AND FOREIGN COUNTRIES
REGISTERED TRADEMARK—MARCA REGISTRADA

MENTOR-UNESCO ART BOOKS ARE PUBLISHED BY
THE NEW AMERICAN LIBRARY, INC.
1301 AVENUE OF THE AMERICAS, NEW YORK, NEW YORK 10019

PRINTED IN ITALY BY AMILCARE PIZZI S.P.A., MILANO

Norwegian churches and museums contain many examples of monumental painting on wood, dating from the thirteenth and fourteenth centuries. For the most part, they consist of altar baldachins and the remains of wall paintings from stave churches (that is, churches built of wood); but there are in addition painted altar frontals which, as their name indicates, used to cover the front of the altars, in both stone and wooden churches. This form of decoration represents an aspect of western European painting of the Middle Ages which has virtually disappeared elsewhere. The fact that Norway is almost the only country in which it has been preserved demands an explanation, and the artistic quality of the works themselves justifies closer study.

When a civil war which had lasted for a century ended about the year 1225, a long era of peace opened in Norway. The country was therefore able to participate in the same vigorous cultural expansion as that experienced by its neighbours bordering on the North Sea. Both Håkon Håkonson (1217-63) and his son Magnus Lagabøter (1263-80) were rulers who gave every encouragement to architecture and the arts generally, and they introduced into their courts a European atmosphere which had never been known in Norway before.

This cultural development was probably due in great measure to a deliberate policy on King Håkon's part. As a patron of the arts, he played a role similar to that of other European princes of that period, such as Henry III of England, Louis IX of France and Frederick II of Germany.

His relations with the English king were particularly cordial, and in the thirteenth century communications with the British Isles multiplied and works of art of many kinds were introduced and produced in Norwegian towns, mainly in what may be called a common Anglo-Norwegian style. Foreign craftsmen settled in Norway and earned a living there, whilst Norwegians went abroad and acquired new ideas and techniques. A truly cosmopolitan atmosphere seems to have developed, most notably in Bergen, where there was a constant stream of visitors from all the Nordic and Baltic states.

This cultural flowering, which was country-wide, can also be attributed in part to the archbishops of Trondheim, although it is difficult nowadays to assess the exact extent of their influence. Summer after summer, pilgrims flocked to the church and shrine of Saint Olav in their hordes. The cathedral had been in the course of construction in the authentic English Early Gothic style since the beginning of the century. Key building workers had been brought in from abroad, especially from Lincoln Cathedral, and nowhere else in Norway was the English style so firmly stamped on the arts in general as in and around Trondheim. In the natural course of events, craftsmen crossed the mountains into eastern Norway, where some of them settled in the bishopric of Hamar in the interior and others reached Oslo on the coast, although in the latter the influence of northern Germany often made itself felt as well. Later still, at the beginning of the second half of the century, the sculptors at Trondheim Cathedral began to adopt the pure High Gothic of Paris, and it was not long before the new style had made its mark in other parts of the country.

It is against this " European " background that the development of monumental paintings must be seen. These made their appearance shortly before the middle of the thirteenth century; as an art form, they seem to have arisen almost spontaneously, for no one looking at their antecedents—the few fragments of Romanesque painting on crosses and on the panel doors of altar shrines—could find any link between them and the altar frontals, baldachins and wall paintings produced in such profusion in the thirteenth and fourteenth centuries.

If we look at thirteenth-century Norwegian painting as a whole, we discover that it consists of three related groupings. First, there are the frescoes on stone. Only a few of these have survived, however, for there were relatively few stone churches, and in many of these the original frescoes were whitewashed over in later years and obliterated. The second group comprises paintings on wood. These are the equivalent in the stave churches of the frescoes on stone. To this same group belong the paintings on the wooden roofs sometimes erected in stone churches above the choir. Lastly there is the third group, the altar frontals. (Mention should perhaps also be made of one more category, that is, book illumination: however, hardly any of these illuminated manuscripts have survived.)

The altar frontals make up by far the most important branch of mediaeval Norwegian painting. They were usually composed of three boards, although occasionally there might be four. The outer surface was planed smooth, but the back was trimmed only roughly with an adze. The edges were dovetailed and then glued. A frame was fixed round the boards to stop them from slipping, and it was common practice for the narrow sides of the framework to extend into a pair of legs which rested on the floor. As a rule the wood was pine, but oak too is found.

As the name tells us, the altar frontal was a decorative finish to the front of the altar, like the more precious examples to be found in other parts of Europe, and of which there are specimens in enamel, silver and mosaic, silver gilt and copper gilt. The thirty-three Norwegian frontals which have endured have a chalk ground, and any knots and cracks in the wood were first pasted over with strips of linen. The panels were decorated with scenes from the life of the saint to whom the altar was dedicated. Elsewhere in countries bordering on the North Sea, only odd specimens of altar decoration remain. There is one in southern Denmark, and an especially noteworthy example from the period about 1180 has survived in Münster (Westphalia). There is another example in Iceland, but generally speaking, no more than fragments have survived here and there in the north of Europe. Apart from Norway, the only country which possesses a considerable number of altar frontals is Spain.

The Spanish frontals date over a much longer period than those in Norway. The majority, including the most valuable, belong to the Romanesque period. They were executed originally not only as paintings on wood but also on stucco and as polychrome wood carvings. The production of paintings on wood, however, was continued right through the High Gothic period.

It is a remarkable coincidence that the only countries which have preserved a sizeable number of altar frontals happen to be two which lie so far apart. At the same time, it would be wrong to assume that this type of panel painting was not just as widespread in most other countries of western Europe. It is significant, for instance, and relevant to the study of Norwegian art, that such paintings had their counterparts in England, and that St. Albans possessed no less than seven in the thirteenth century. If so many happen to have survived in Norway, the main reason must be sought in the centuries of economic difficulties which followed the devastation of the great plague in the fourteenth century, and the serious misgovernment by a series of successive rulers.

The altar frontals which are still in existence have been discovered in almost every region of Norway, as far north as Tromsø on the Arctic Ocean. Most of them, however, come from the churches in the province of Sogn in the west, presumably because the curators of the Historisk Museum in Bergen recognized their value during the first half of the nineteenth century and began to collect and safeguard them. In one church no fewer than three specimens were found, and several others contributed two each. A stone church in eastern Norway also contained three.

The measurements of these altar frontals, which were usually one to two metres in width and about one metre high, place them in the category of panel paintings. They give us an insight into a contemporary genre which may

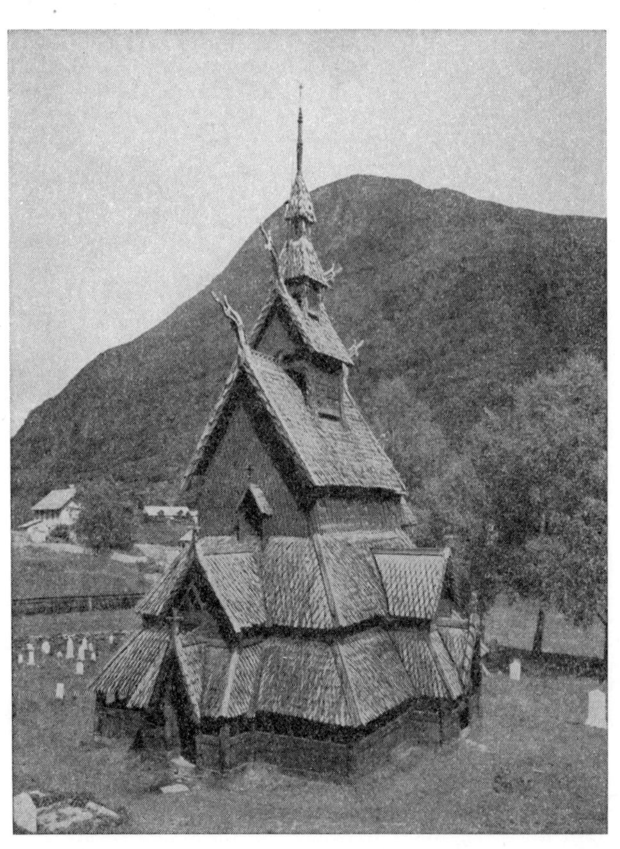

Borgund stave church. c. 1150.

be compared with stained glass, book illumination and frescoes. Just as these different art forms had their specialists who copied freely from one another in a fertile interchange of ideas, so did panel painting have its masters who left their mark on the medium, and like artists in other fields, they learned how to adapt their technique to its specific purpose. We see this not least in their draughtsmanship, in the powerful curves and the treatment of drapery, and in other details which were not possible in, say, manuscript illustration, but which became absolutely essential here on account of the larger format.

If we attempt to pick out definite schools or individual masters in Norwegian art, we at once run into difficulties. After all, what has survived can only be a small fraction of the total. All the same, we can differentiate between the three main regions, although even here the dividing lines are blurred in terms of both the finished products and the master painters. Bergen in the west may be considered the main centre of altar frontal painting. Trondheim, the spiritual capital, also had its workshops, which showed time and again how skilfully they could exploit the latest trends introduced by the constant stream of new craftsmen, such as glass painters and sculptors, employed in building the cathedral. For the third region, eastern Norway, it is more difficult to find a focal point, for here there were several towns in which skilled crafts-men settled—the bishopric of Hamar inland, Oslo and the ancient trading centre of Tønsberg on the coast.

Among the laws which Magnus Lagabøter drew up for the administration of the town of Bergen, we find one that restricted painters to a certain quarter of the town near the main thoroughfare. The works which are pre-served confirm that these painters followed the technical principles which Theophilus Presbyter had laid down for craftsmen in Germany a couple of centuries earlier and which were common throughout Europe. An Icelandic painting manual, which probably originated in Bergen, recommended that a chalk ground should be applied in several coats. Next, it should be overlaid with silver and smoothed down with wolf's or dog's teeth and allowed to dry in the sun. Patterns might be engraved in the silver, or in the chalk base. Gold should be laid over the silver. A " more economical " method, however, was to apply an oil-based glaze, which would give the effect of gilding. In Paris, where the standards of workmanship were regulated by the guild, such sharp practice would have been severely punished; but in Norway no one exercised effective control.

However, it must be conceded that painters were already anticipating one major development in technique. An analysis of various altar frontals and painted statues has shown that the colours were mixed with some kind of oil. The Icelandic manual also mentions oil, as we have seen. Of course, this was not yet oil painting as pioneered by the brothers Van Eyck, but all the same, the use of oil must already have acquired a certain importance by this time.

The thirteenth and fourteenth centuries were the great epoch for the cult of the Virgin, and many poets from western Nordic countries sang her hymns of praise. The Madonna is the moon which receives her light from the sun, that is, her son Jesus. She is the *stella maris*, the star of the sea, and there are many other allusions which show her great significance for the religious life of the time. The King of Heaven and Lord of the Sun, is, of course, Christ, and this is the theme to which the earliest of the altar frontals are devoted. The one from Ulvik church in Hardanger, over 80 cm in height, shows a figure of Christ Enthroned (Plate 1). Round him stand the twelve Apostles; they are of humbler stature and most of them are engaged in animated conversation. Only the four figures standing nearest to Christ are looking up at him. The whole picture has a gold background, engraved with a leaf pattern, and this throws into relief the red mandorla framework around Our Lord and the red trefoil arches above each of the Apostles. The varied tones of red, blue, green and brown in the robes and in the framework give the effect of an enamelled sheen, which may have been intentional.

Both in style and subject we see here a typical English

Early Gothic painting from the middle of the century, which is not at all surprising when we think of the close ties between the two countries. In this instance, there are similarities with English sources ranging from the first three decades of the century, with the stocky figures and gilded backgrounds of the *Lothian Bible* (New York, Pierpont Morgan Library, MS. 791), to a period nearer the middle of the century with the *Amesbury Psalter* (Oxford, All Souls College, MS. 6).

Many new and stimulating forces reached Norwegian towns in the first half of the century, not only through the visits of foreign artists like Matthew Paris, who came to Bergen and Trondheim in 1248, but also through the introduction of illuminated manuscripts from England and France. Other influences may have been exerted by those Norwegians who returned from abroad after mastering new skills. These dynamic movements left their most beautiful imprint in the altar frontals painted during the 1260s. The calligraphic flow of line which Matthew Paris adopted in the middle of the thirteenth century can best be seen in a life-size Saint Peter, in off-white against a red background, painted on the door of an altar shrine from the church at Fåberg in eastern Norway. This English calligraphic line recurs both in a very beautiful contemporary altar frontal from Hauge church in Sogn, and also in a rather badly damaged frontal from Kaupanger stave church on the same fjord. The circular panels of the Hauge church, which represent the Crucifixion with white figures against a red or a green background, are exquisite. As so often in Norwegian painting, we find that the best parallels for figures of Christ crucified are in the lyrically felt lines of the carved and painted crucifixes, which are often well preserved.

Meanwhile, the cultural climate in Bergen had proved so fertile that several art forms were able to develop simultaneously. The calligraphic style of figure drawing becomes less important and is replaced by one which includes both the Ulvik frontal and a distinctive panel from the stone church at Kinsarvik on the Hardanger Fjord. The mandorla-shaped border around the Crucifixion group in the centre is the same as that in the Hauge altar frontal; however, the gathering below the Cross is not only much bigger but also contains realistic detail which is wholly absent from the first panel. The faces are broad, the figures stocky, and to indicate that this is an object of devotion and not merely a historical representation, Peter and Paul are present at the Cross too. In addition, the play of line is much richer and the artist has used his colours to create shadows and thereby give an effect of depth.

The most important example of this tendency is without doubt a fragment of a panel from Fet church in Sogn. It includes the Annunciation (Plate 3) and the birth of Christ (although this may have been one of a pair of doors from a shrine devoted to the Madonna). From the style, it seems certain that this work of art belongs to the second half of the century, that is, to a period when the French High Gothic was beginning to make itself felt, and slim body proportions were often swathed in massed drapery.

In eastern Norway, the oldest examples we have belong to the same period as those in western Norway. The calligraphically executed figure of Saint Peter at Fåberg has already been mentioned. Much richer, and at least as old, is the magnificent altar frontal from Heddal stave church in Telemark (Plate 2). Its size indicates that it was created for the high altar of the church, and since the altar can be classified from its style as belonging to the period about 1250, there is every reason to believe that this frontal was commissioned for the consecration of the church. Heddal church is the biggest stave church standing today and it stands out like a cathedral, dominating the valley.

Again we have a powerful figure of Christ Enthroned, with his right hand raised in blessing. The Apostles, discussing and gesticulating, are arranged in groups of three and form two rows, one on either side, each spanned by a wide arch. As in the case of the Ulvik frontal the background here is gold, but for the rest there is a much richer use of colour. The range is from deep

turquoise to pale blue and green, from the dark red of
the borders and dividing lines, to a delicate pink in the
treatment of the beard. The cloak which Christ wears
and some of the Apostles' robes are a deep crimson.
Many features link this work with the East Anglian style,
in particular an Apocalypse from roughly 1230, which was
probably executed at St. Albans and is now at Trinity
College, Cambridge. In the treatment of the head, especially that of the eyes and beard, there is a striking resemblance between this presentation of Christ and the heads
of kings painted by Matthew Paris and other painters
about the middle of the century, which can be seen both
in the frescoes at Windsor Castle and in the *Chronica
Minora* at Corpus Christi College, Cambridge.

Another panel painting in the same tradition is a well
preserved altar frontal of the Madonna which belongs to
the period nearer the end of the century. It adorned the
high altar in Tingelstad church in Hadeland (Plate 4).
It is one of the oldest surviving Madonna frontals, and
heralds numerous similar works to the glory of the
Virgin Mary painted from approximately 1300 until well
into the fourteenth century, and found in all parts of
the country. Perhaps there is a faint link between the
painter of the Heddal altar frontal and the somewhat
later artist who was responsible for the baldachin paintings in the Torpo stave church reproduced in Plates
16 to 20.

Of the thirteenth-century paintings in the archbishopric
of Trondheim, we know very little. We may assume that
they did in fact exist from the study of other works of
art which have endured, such as painted altar sculptures
and crucifixes in delicate styles, both Early and High
Anglo-Norwegian Gothic. At the same period the many
windows in the octagon, the choir and the nave must
necessarily have been filled with stained glass. Within
the bishopric of Trondheim, we find an example of the
influence exerted by the stained glass masters in the
completed quatrefoil sections of an altar frontal in Eid
church in Romsdal which belongs to the beginning of
the fourteenth century. Two altar frontals, both in good

condition, one from Kvaefjord in Tromsø in the north and the other from Holtålen (?) in Trøndelag, show that the High Gothic style flourished in these parts in the middle of the fourteenth century. The latter is, moreover, the sole remaining altar frontal which is devoted to Saint Olav, Norway's patron saint and king, and the ancestor of its monarchs.

About the year 1300, King Håkon V, who was passionately interested in all things French, moved his royal palace from Bergen in the west to Oslo in the east, and this move must undoubtedly have had a strong effect on the artistic life there. A little of this can be seen in the bisected altar frontal in the church of Tingelstad, and rather more powerfully in the " beheaded " frontal of Ulnes in Valdres. But there is so little material left and what there is, is in such a poor state of preservation, that we are not entitled to deduce much from it. All we can say is that the painting here too followed the general European trend into the High Gothic.

In Bergen, the capital of Håkon Håkonson and Magnus Lagabøter, the art of panel painting was continued by painters who were in the forefront of the new movements. At least, the material which has survived indicates that this was so in the first decade of the new century, although already there are signs of a certain degree of provincialism, which became inevitable once the artist was no longer working under the eye of his sovereign.

Pride of place must go to a Madonna frontal in good condition from Odda church, deep inland on the Hardanger Fjord. The width of the panel suggests that in all probability it covered the front of the high altar, and we may also infer from this that the church was dedicated to the Virgin. A blissfully smiling Madonna sits fair and square on a bench (Plate 5). Her dress is red and a shimmering dark green cloak is draped round it in ample folds. On her left knee sits the infant Jesus wearing a little green robe, stretching out his right hand towards a dove perched on a twig held by Mary in her right hand. Around the picture itself there is a framework of delicate construction, and above the slopes of a gabled arch are two iridescent angels' wings, in shimmering reds on one side and in greens shading to blue on the other. The background is gold, with fillets and frameworks in varied tones of green, red, beige and white.

The lavish use of rich colour recurs in the four scenes which narrate the story of Mary's life. These show us in turn: Mary's birth; Joachim and Anne being parted; Mary as a child on the steps leading to the Temple; and finally Mary's three suitors, facing the High Priest, with Joseph the carpenter holding in his hand a staff which is sprouting green leaves (Plate 6).

Taking the North Sea area in 1300 as a whole, this frontal must rank as one of its finest examples. The draughtsmanship is spacious and assured. The choice of colour and the modelling of the shadows represents a chromatic zenith for Norwegian painting of the Middle Ages. Certainly it is not the exquisite, almost affected elegance of the Paris and Cologne schools, or the English " royal " style that we see here. But it may be true to say that these Odda panels show the beginnings of a reaction by the " peripheral " artists against the over-refined and unlifelike tendencies at the principal centres. A similar reaction took place elsewhere, as we can see in the works of the stained glass craftsmen in the cathedrals of northern France, in some of the churches in the Rhineland, and in English provincial art.

The Odda panel, however, does not stand alone. Much of its colour range can be found in a well preserved altar frontal in Tresfjord church in Romsdal, and indeed, it may well have been produced in the same workshop. It shows an identical use of colour to create the effect of depth, and these two paintings may be said to form a complete little school of their own.

Side by side with it, we may place the Saint Botolph panel from Årdal stave church in Sogn (Plate 7), which owes much to the English influence. It is quieter in the effect of its media and might be considered nearer the style of " royal " Norwegian art, if the concept is not too fanciful. On the same level stands the highly detailed altar frontal from Nedstryn stave church in Nordfjord

(Plate 8). The painted medallions tell of King Chosroes and the Holy Cross, and how the Emperor Heraclius eventually killed Chosroes and brought back the Cross to Jerusalem. The old Norse inscription to the scene reproduced, reads as follows: " I, King Heraclius, arrive at the strong citadel of Jerusalem, but blinded by vanity, he [*sic*] cannot see the city's gate."

The tendency of provincial art towards both exaggeration and realism emerges strongly in two altar frontals, representing the Madonna and the Crucifixion, from Nes stave church in Sogn, painted at the beginning of the fourteenth century. The Madonna frontal is a truly delightful picture with a plump, smiling Christ child wriggling on his mother's lap and pointing a chubby finger imperiously at something he wants (Plate 9). It is faintly reminiscent of Japanese painting of much more recent times. The bearing of the Three Wise Men in the Adoration of the Magi (Plate 10) from the same altar frontal is certainly regal, yet the effect is positively comic as one of them raises his crown in greeting, with a surprised expression on his face. The relationship between these two works and the Tresfjord panel is unmistakable and can be seen most clearly in the Christ child and the picture of the Magi. Obviously this panel was painted by an apprentice.

The Crucifixion altar frontal (Plates 11 to 13) has lost almost all its gilded glaze, so that the silver underlay is exposed and gives the texture a different appearance from the one intended. In the way the scene is split up, however, and in the grouping of the main figures, the artist is breaking new ground. Only Mary and John pose in the traditional manner, as a sign of their emotion. On and around the ladders, small figures are bustling about, busy with their hammers and pincers, and thus bringing vividly to life the words of the ancient Passion poet from the west of Norway: " Loud rang the blows of the hammer as they nailed Christ, the chieftain, to the cross." As a work of art, this panel must rank as the finest of all the Crucifixion frontals in the High Gothic style, and this assessment is due much more to its intrinsic merit, than to the fact that it happens to be the best preserved of them all.

Later developments tend to become more stereotyped, as can be seen in one of the altar frontals from Dale church in Sogn. In the Annunciation, we recognize once more the extravagantly elongated figures like those in contemporary stained glass windows (Plate 14). This feature is found, too, in the altar frontal from Røldal in Hordaland, which shows Christ at the Gates of Hell (Plate 15). Judging by its measurements, this must have come from a side altar. The use of colouring is less sophisticated, the pigments themselves are poorer in quality and the draughtsmanship shows a decided leaning towards an expressionist simplification. From this frontal to the baldachin at Årdal (Plates 27 and 28), it is artistically speaking only a short step. There is no doubt that the Trondheim school, as exemplified in the huge standing figures of the Kvaefjord altar frontal and the Olav frontal from Holtålen (?), represent later Gothic panel painting at its best.

If we leave aside the vaulted roof above the choir in Vestre Slidre church in Valdres, then all the wall and ceiling paintings on wood have come to us from the stave churches. The walls of these churches were eminently suitable for painting, for the big windowless surfaces were unbroken on both sides except for the doorways. The ceilings, on the contrary, did not allow any opportunity for decoration on account of their construction. The first impression inside a stave church is one of almost complete darkness. Then a wealth of detail begins to emerge in the trickle of light which filters through the small round holes at the height of the triforium. If the door is left open, as it commonly was in summer, then the whole space is lit up. The modest floor dimensions, coupled with the considerable height, give these churches a remarkably personal and intimate effect and the texture of the wood adds warmth to the whole.

There is no reason to believe that the interior of the stave churches were intended to be painted. On the

18

contrary, it was probably customary in the early days to hang textiles on the walls, tapestries narrating scenes from the sagas, mythology or the Bible.

Of greater interest to us today are the antique ciboria or baldachins. In Italy, one finds a certain number carved in stone, which bear a resemblance to those in Norway, for instance to the ciborium in the stave church at Hopperstad. Painted church ceilings are found elsewhere in Europe in large numbers, but they have no connexion with the barrel-arched ciborium roof, which is a sub-structure resting on pillars in the middle of the nave, as in Torpo and Ål in Hallingdal or in Vang in Valdres. They must surely have also existed widely elsewhere in Norway, and were destroyed when the stave churches were pulled down or rebuilt. As far as both period and function are concerned there are also certain flat baldachins in Spain which can be classified with that in Årdal stave church, in spite of the difference in their shape.

The real reason why a number of Norwegian churches have the ciborium roof to the east of the central nave must lie in a specific liturgical precept, in the erection of altars in honour of the Holy Cross or the Holy Rood. One of the motivating forces may be found in French practice, for as we saw above there were close relations between the Norwegian kings and the French rulers, who were the custodians of the holy relic, the crown of thorns, in Paris. Like Louis IX, Håkon Håkonson and his successors also founded chapels royal, and in 1274 Magnus Lagabøter received one of the thorns from the crown. The church he had built in Bergen to house the sacred relic was considerably influenced by the Sainte-Chapelle.

From the point of view of technique, the canopy paintings and the wall paintings on wood form a category of their own within the more general classification of monumental painting. The pigment was applied over a chalk ground, which was so thin that the paint was almost forced into the wood. Unevenness and small cracks were ignored. Probably this method—developed through working on such large surfaces—made a virtue of necessity. It has certainly had the effect of preserving

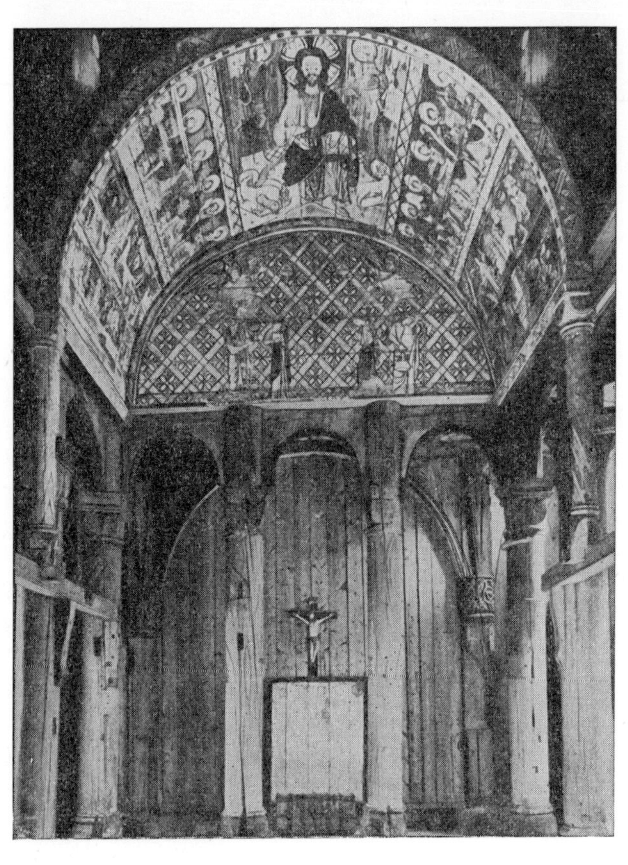

*Interior of Torpo stave church, Hallingdal. The painted vaulting.
Middle of the thirteenth century.*

the paintings exceptionally well. It is fairly safe to assert that these pictures were the work of master painters who understood the art of fresco painting, as the two techniques are to some degree related.

The oldest painted ceilings are still to be found in their original position in Torpo stave church in Hallingdal. The roof is open to the west. To the east are the figures of Mary, John, Ecclesia (the Church) and Synagogue, as well as angels swinging censers above a space which is now empty, but which must once have been occupied by a carved crucifix. There are still the marks of the nails to show where it hung. In the centre of the vaulted arch, a powerful Christ is enthroned against a background which is divided in two and sprinkled with stars (Plate 16). His feet stand firmly on a green mound of earth and in the corners are placed the symbols of the Four Evangelists.

To left and right of the central figure the design is balanced, so that we have two rows of Apostles facing each other in a central panel on either side. They are either looking up at Our Lord or else are deep in animated discussion of sacred subjects (Plate 18). All are tonsured as if they were monks. Two of them carry the symbols of the keys and the sword and so can be identified as Peter and Paul (the latter was frequently represented with the Disciples). Two further panels on each side depict the martyrdom of the popular Saint Margaret of Antioch (Plates 17, 19 and 20).

The ceiling is strangely effective, hanging as it does high above the heads of the congregation. The blue tones and the strong unbroken reds both dominate and integrate the composition. The gilded areas provide the third main colour tone, whilst pleasing middle tones are added by the use of brown dividing lines or stylized tendrils, and greenish diamond shapes filled in with a delicate cross pattern. The figures themselves are powerfully stylized, although the treatment here is not as thoroughgoing as that of Christ's countenance, which seems to be deliberately archaic. All the contours and folds are strongly emphasized with black or occasionally red outlines. The observer has good reason to be reminded of European stained glass, where the same means were freely used to produce a similar effect.

A man like the painter of Torpo must have been restricted to the environment of a town, possibly the bishopric of Hamar deep in the interior, where new movements would take longest to infiltrate. But there, just as elsewhere in Europe, he must have produced his sketch-book and worked out the best way to reconcile the various conflicting wishes he was expected to gratify.

The same problems must also have confronted his fellow artists a little later in the century at the neighbouring church of Ål, some six miles to the north in the same valley. Here was built an outstandingly beautiful stave church dating from the period 1160 to 1170, which survived until about 1880. In the second half of the thirteenth century, the church was extended in the east and an exceptionally large baldachin was added. At the same time, part of the walls of the nave were decorated with scenes completing the narrative started on the ceiling.

The church ceiling in Ål was enclosed not only to the east, but also to the west. Unlike Torpo church, it must have had the effect of an enormous illustrated Bible, for the wording of the scriptures is closely followed in scene after scene. In a circular panel in the middle of the ceiling appears the Creation of Heaven and Earth and all living things, beginning with the idyllic life of Adam and Eve in the Garden of Eden (Plate 21). Architectonically framed, the story is continued in two friezes, one on either side. The Serpent in Paradise (Plate 22), the workaday life that followed the Fall, the Annunciation, the meeting between Mary and Elizabeth (Plate 23), the birth of Jesus, the Adoration of the Magi (Plate 24), the Flight into Egypt (Plate 25), the Vision of Herod and the Slaughter of the Innocents at Bethlehem. Stretching across the whole of the west wall was a painting of one of the cardinal events in the New Testament, the Last Supper. Then there follows the Washing of the Feet, the arrest in the Garden of Gethsemane, the Scourging and the Way to the Cross until the focal point is reached: the

Crucifixion, the epitome of the Christian faith. This Crucifixion, which occupied the whole of the eastern wall above the high altar (Plate 26), has a background filled in with diagonal cruciform patterns in red. Against it, we have a superbly stylized figure of Christ on a green cross, with bejewelled tips and edges to the upright and the arms. At the foot of the cross are Mary, John, Stephaton and Longinus, as well as Ecclesia Triumphant and the defeated Synagogue with the head of the scapegoat in her hands. The remaining panels deal with the Resurrection, the Women by the Graveside, and Christ's Descent into Hell from which he rescues the lost souls, led by Adam and Eve.

Of all the baldachins that have come down to us, the one from Ål is by far the most important. The paintings from Vang in the neighbouring valley of Valdres have disappeared, but they were almost High Gothic in style and, from the point of view of iconography, they seem to have combined features from both Torpo and Ål. The altar canopy from Årdal in Sogn, on the other hand, with its appealing simplification of colour and design, must have belonged more to the folk art of the Middle Ages (Plates 27 and 28).

Here and there, it seems that the painter of Ål has allowed himself a considerable degree of freedom in arrangement. He jumps from one subject to another, and gives the impression that he must have got a few pages of his sketch-book mixed up. He had a much more varied palette at his disposal than the other ceiling painters and probably he owed this to a close acquaintance with miniature and altar frontal painters. His green tones predominate, but there are many other colours used, including black which is very rare elsewhere, and which is lavishly applied in this instance.

Whilst the paintings at Torpo stand out today as more or less unique in Norwegian art, these at Ål are stylistically related to religious wooden sculpture, and a large number of crucifixes of a similar type have been preserved. They belong to a style and an iconography which, broadly speaking, originated in the English school and, as one would readily suppose, they reached eastern Norway via the archbishopric of Trondheim or by way of the sea. But here more than anywhere, one has the feeling that some clues are missing. Perhaps Low German art exerted its influence here about the middle of the century, as it did on the wooden sculptures in eastern Norway.

There is no doubt at all that any study of the history of Norwegian Gothic painting must be set against the background of the whole of the area bordering on the North Sea. In Norwegian towns, many influences mingled and the result is often painting of a character which is just as original as the oil painting technique which the masters used for their altar frontals. Although in certain respects, this genre may be said to exhibit certain properties of peripheral art, there is little evidence for dismissing it as basically a retarded art form. On the contrary, these paintings reveal an astonishing familiarity with the main streams of cultural development in the principal centres round the North Sea. As in Viking times, the North Sea was a vital artery of communication and this traffic affected artists who were specifically church painters, no matter whether they worked on wood or on plaster.

If we confine ourselves to the material which has been preserved to the present day in the form of altar frontals, baldachins and wall paintings from both stone and wooden churches, then the span of Norwegian painting is not much more than a hundred years in all. It developed from the optimistic and progressive Early Gothic of the first half of the thirteenth century under the patronage of kings as well as that of the Church. In the difficult and troubled times which followed the extinction of the old royal house in 1319, and the devastation caused by the plague that swept the country in 1348, Norwegian art collapsed and disappeared. But before that happened, works of art were created which, by a stroke of chance, were destined to reveal many aspects of western European monumental painting of the thirteenth and fourteenth centuries that would otherwise have remained unknown.

ILLUSTRATIONS

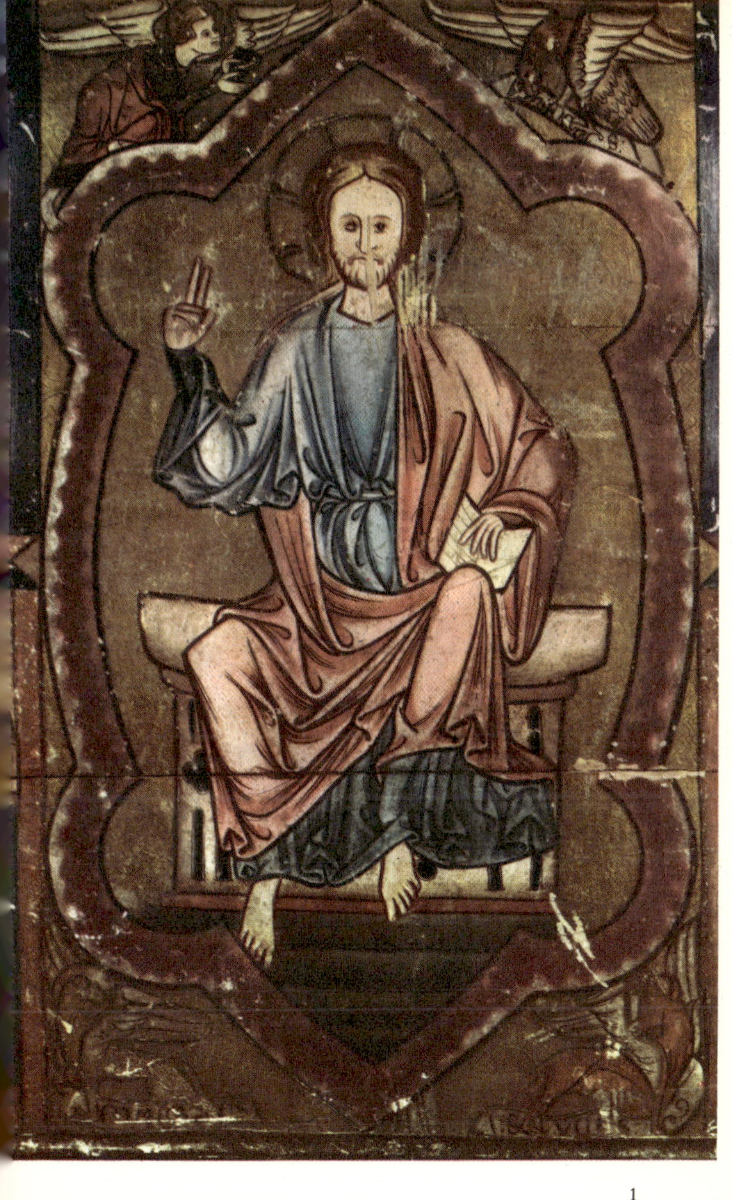

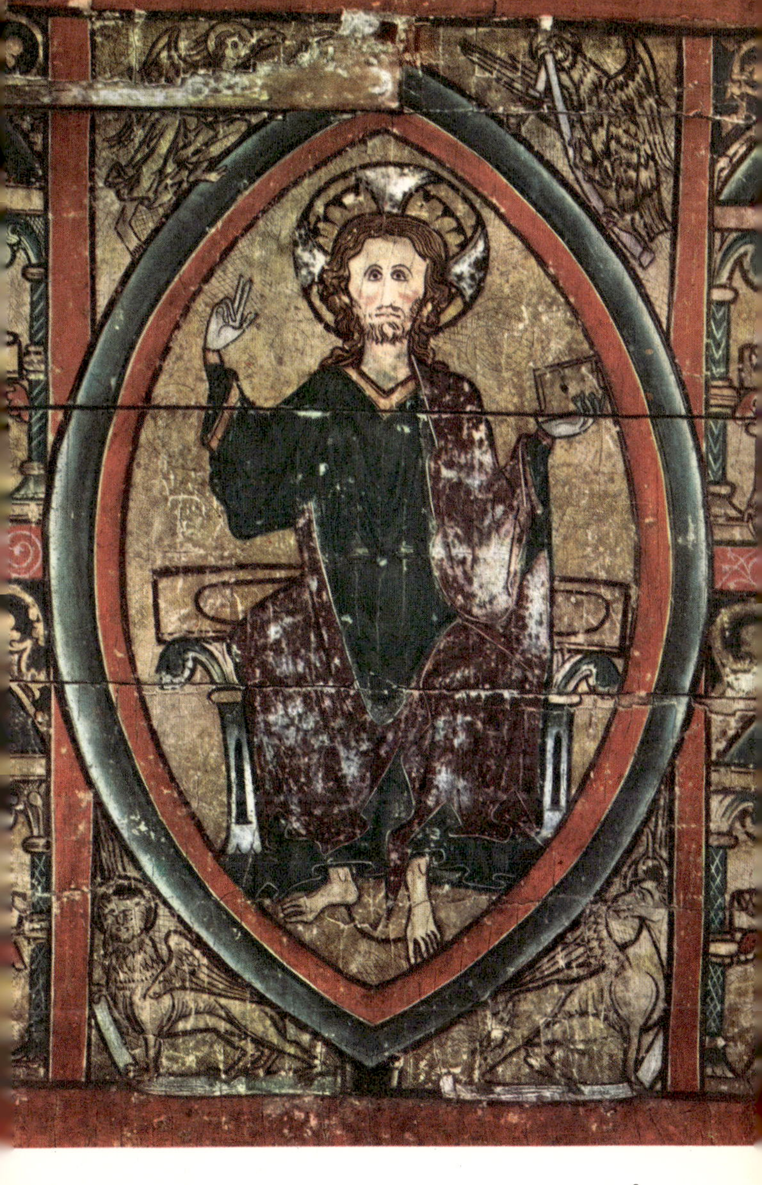

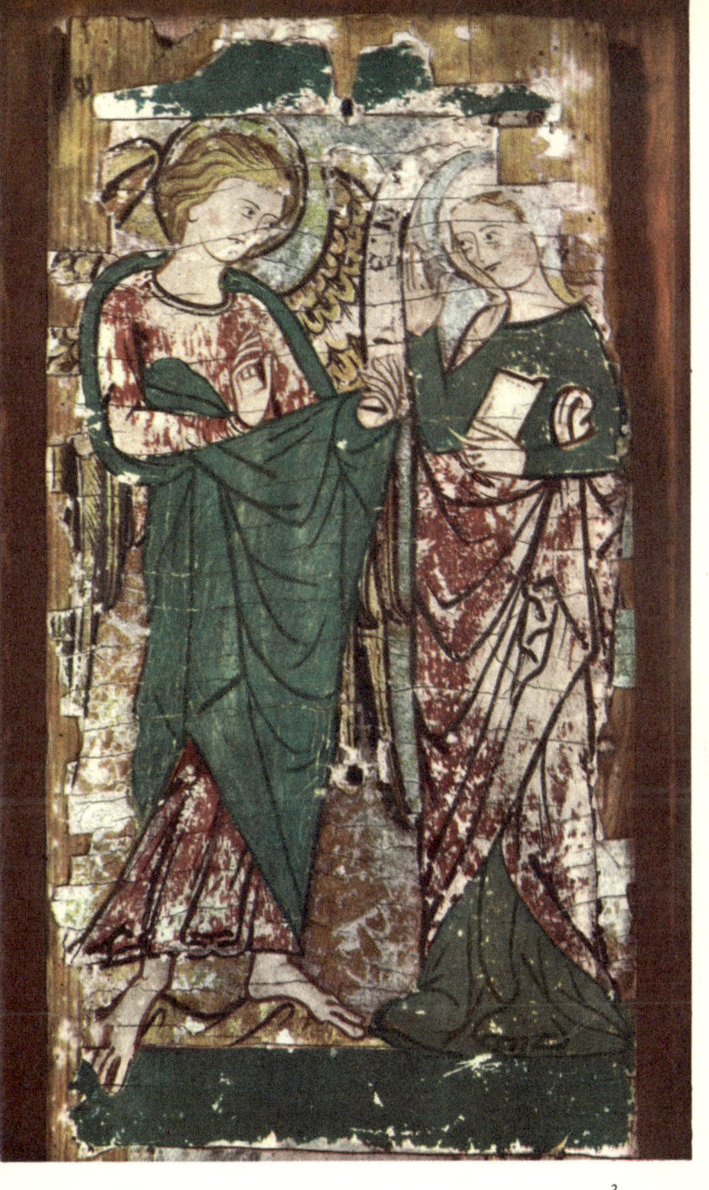

3

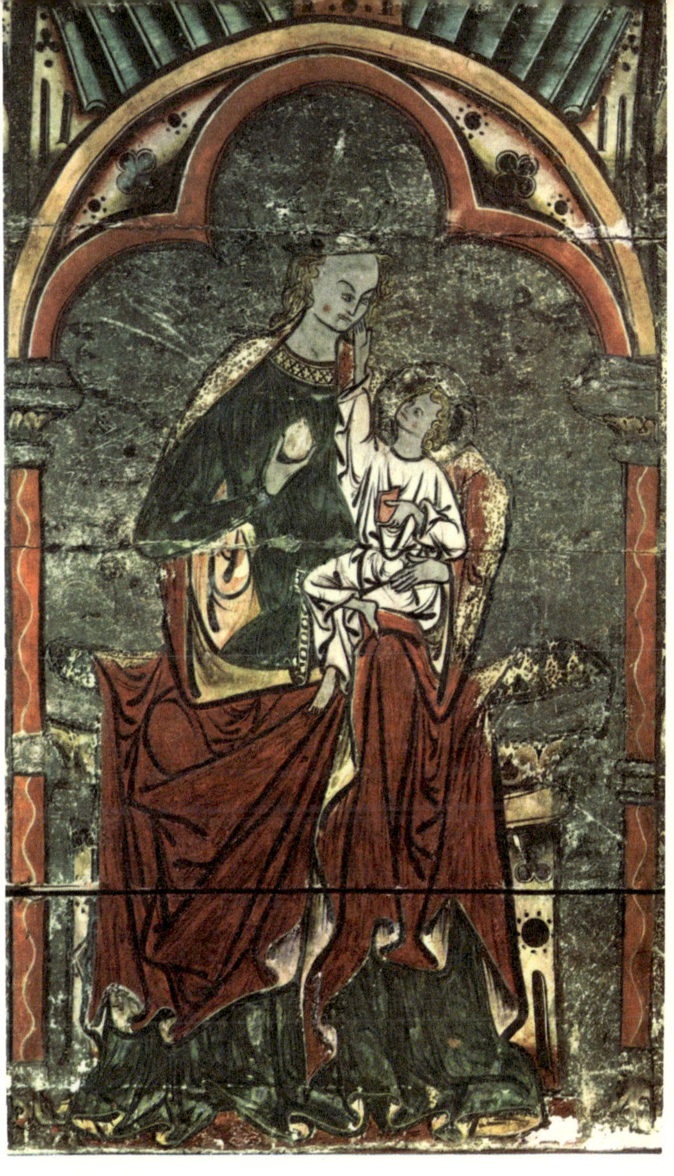

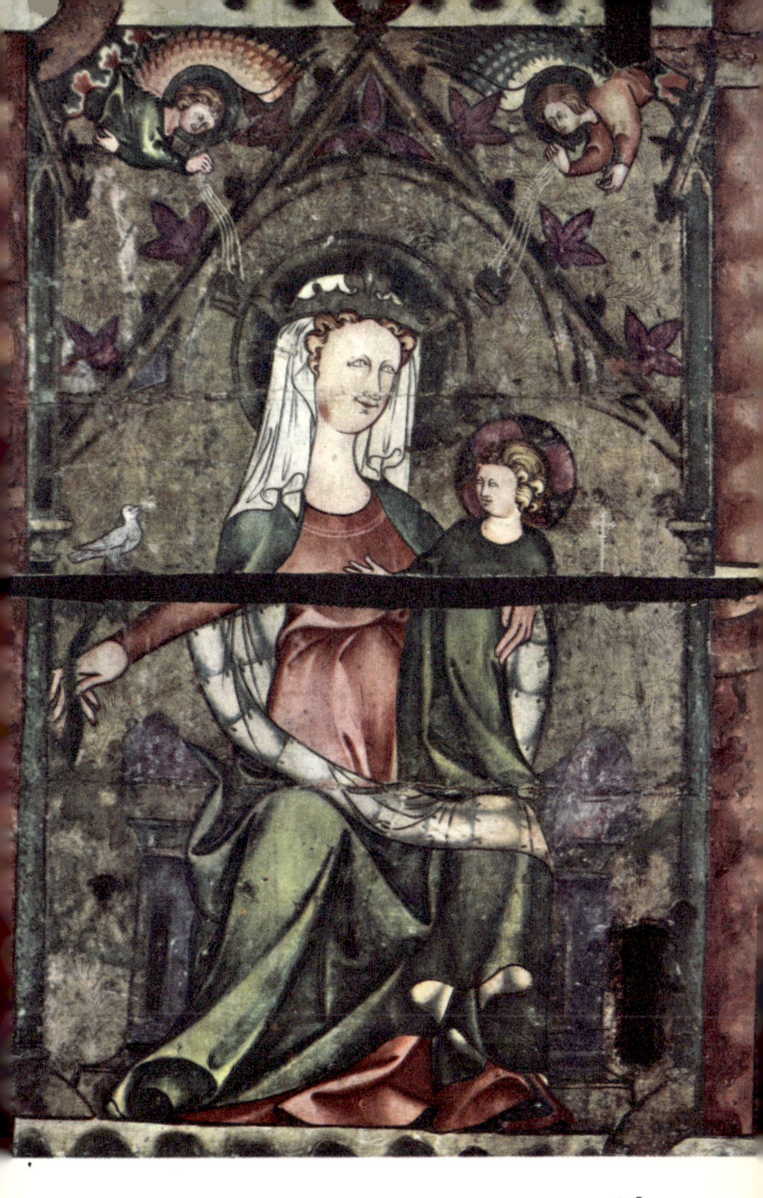

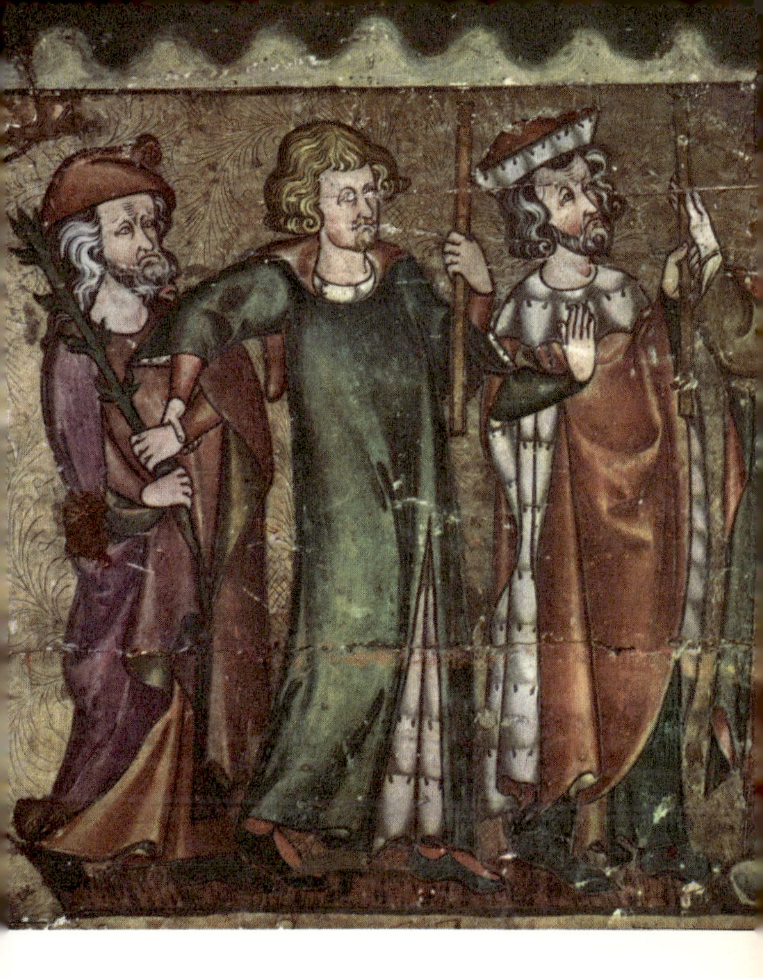

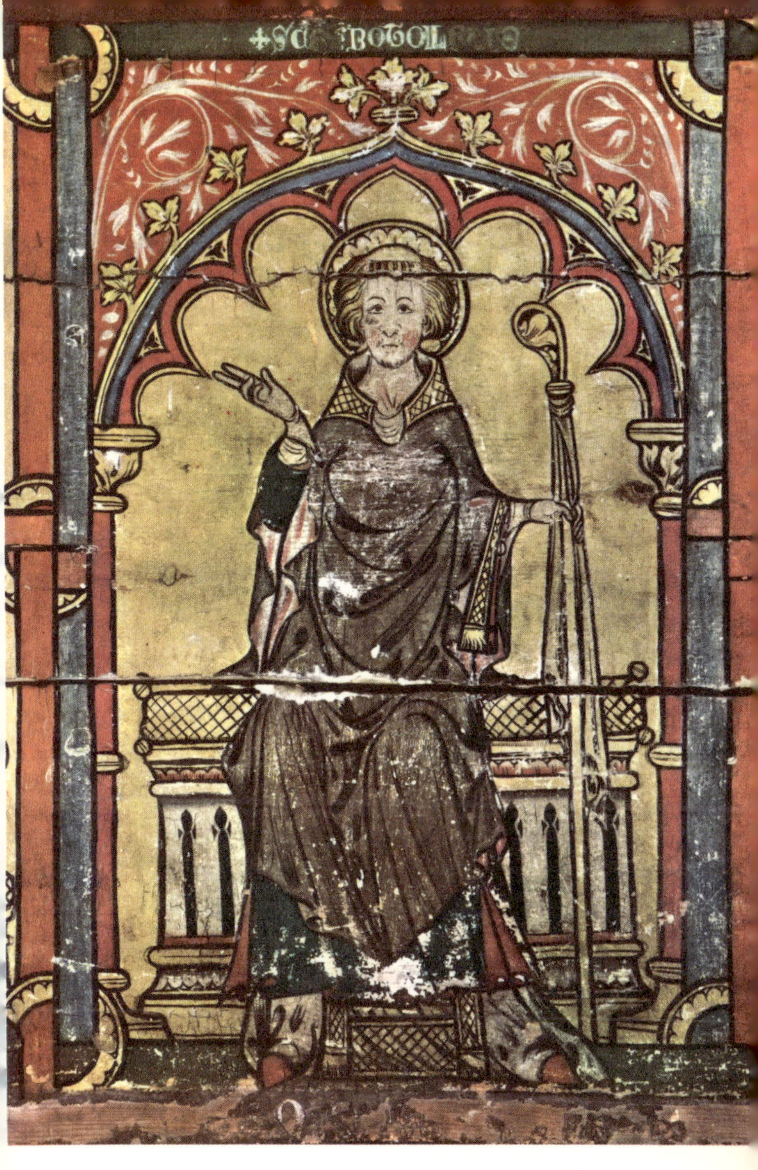
✠ SCS ꝛ BOTOL

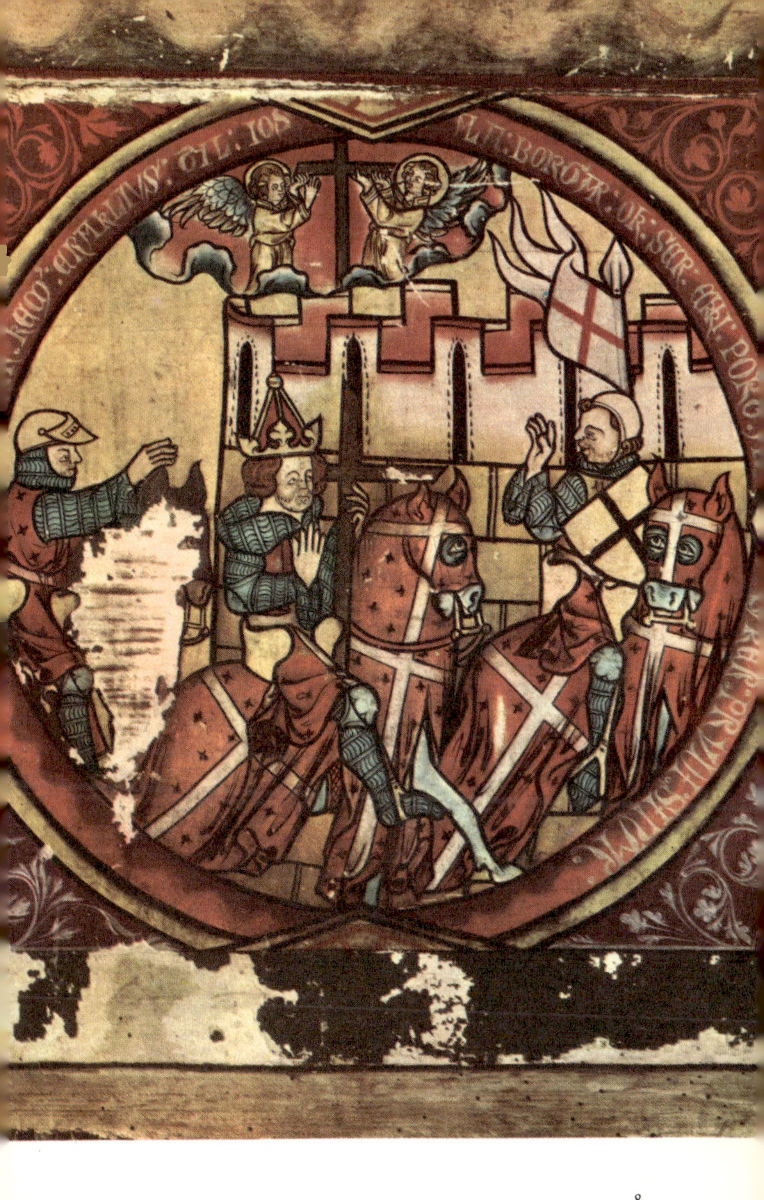

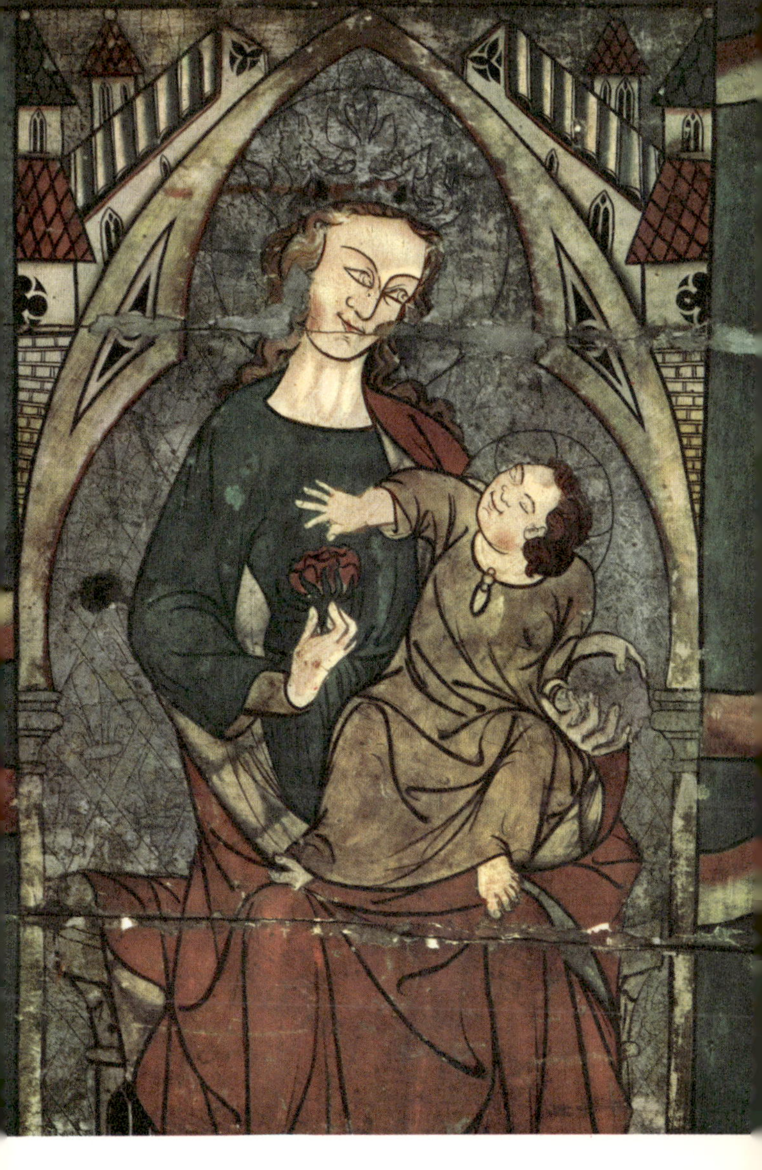

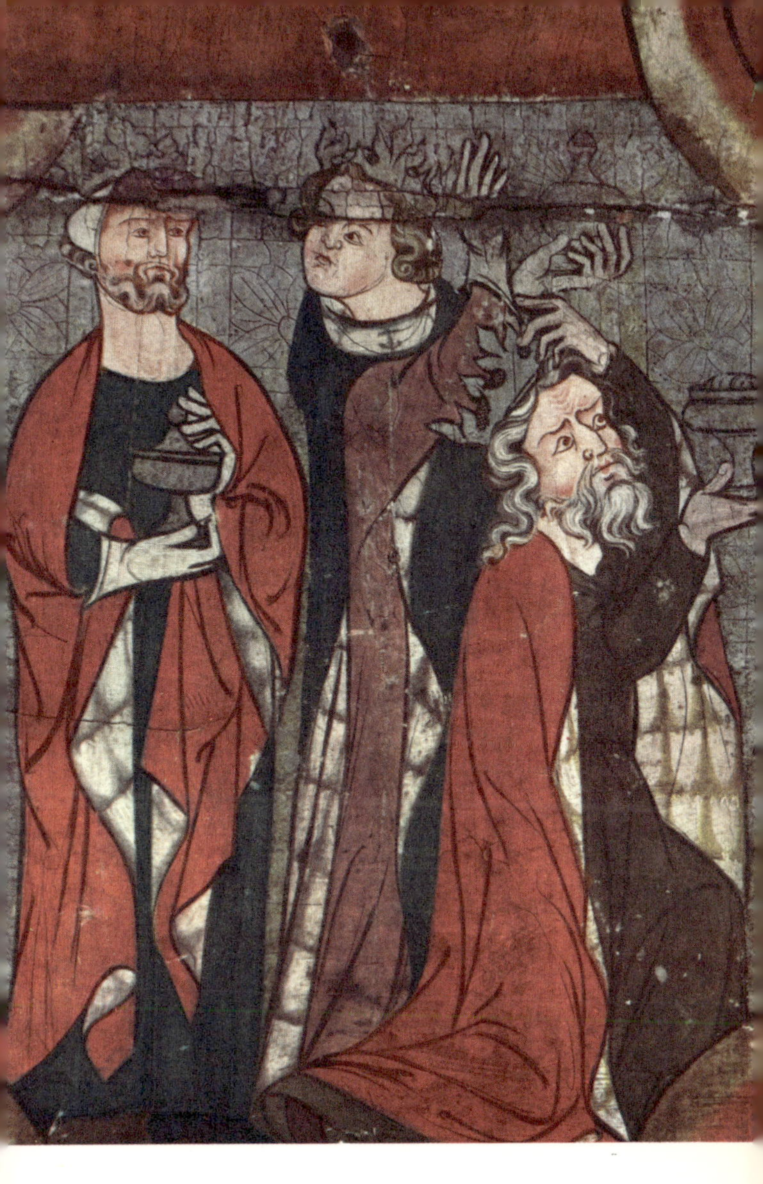

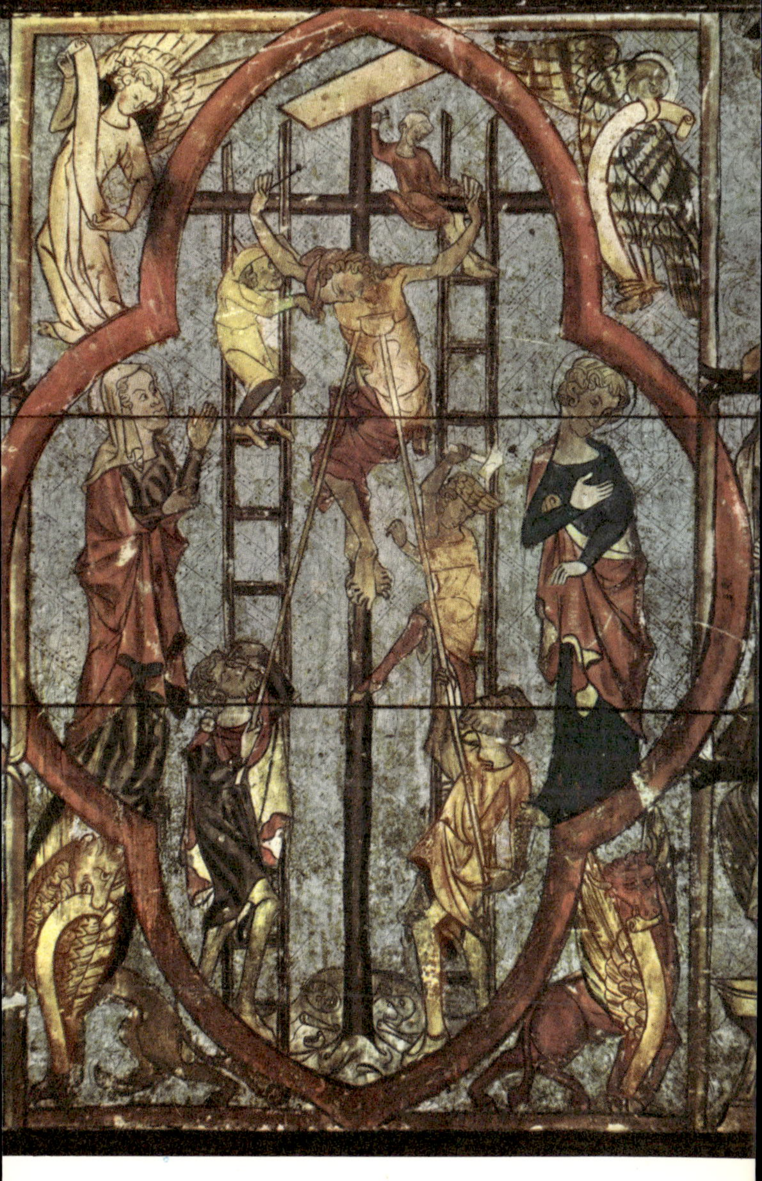

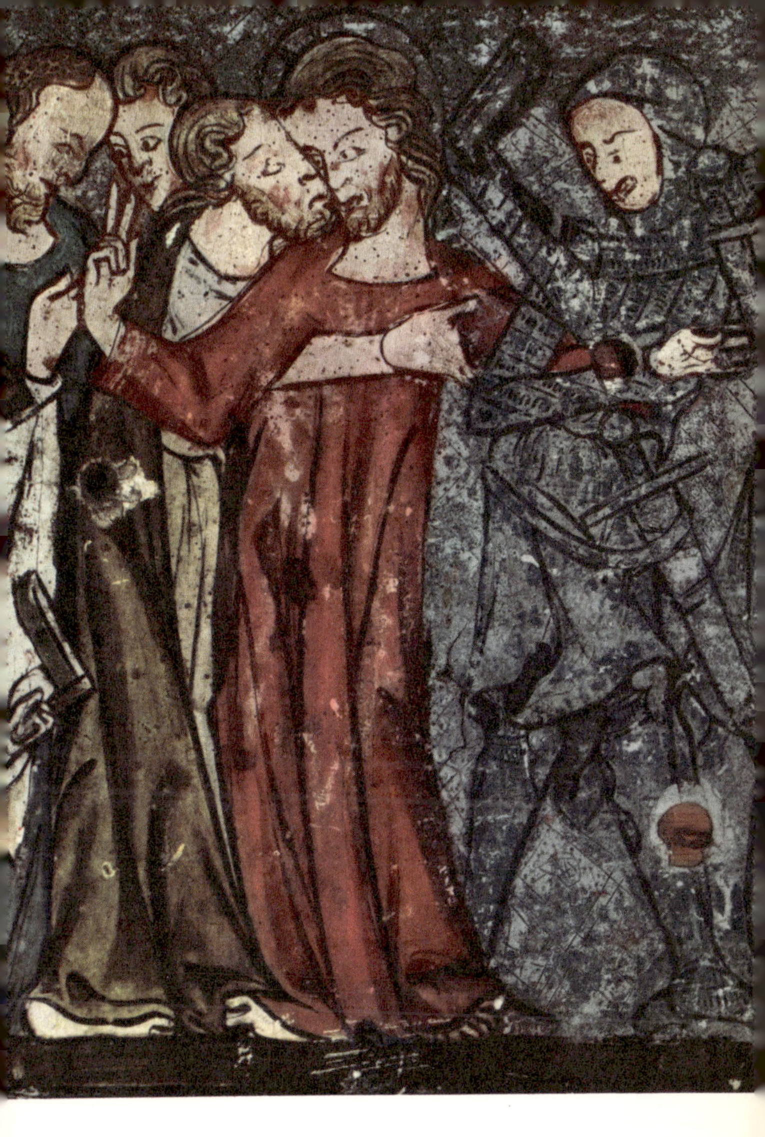

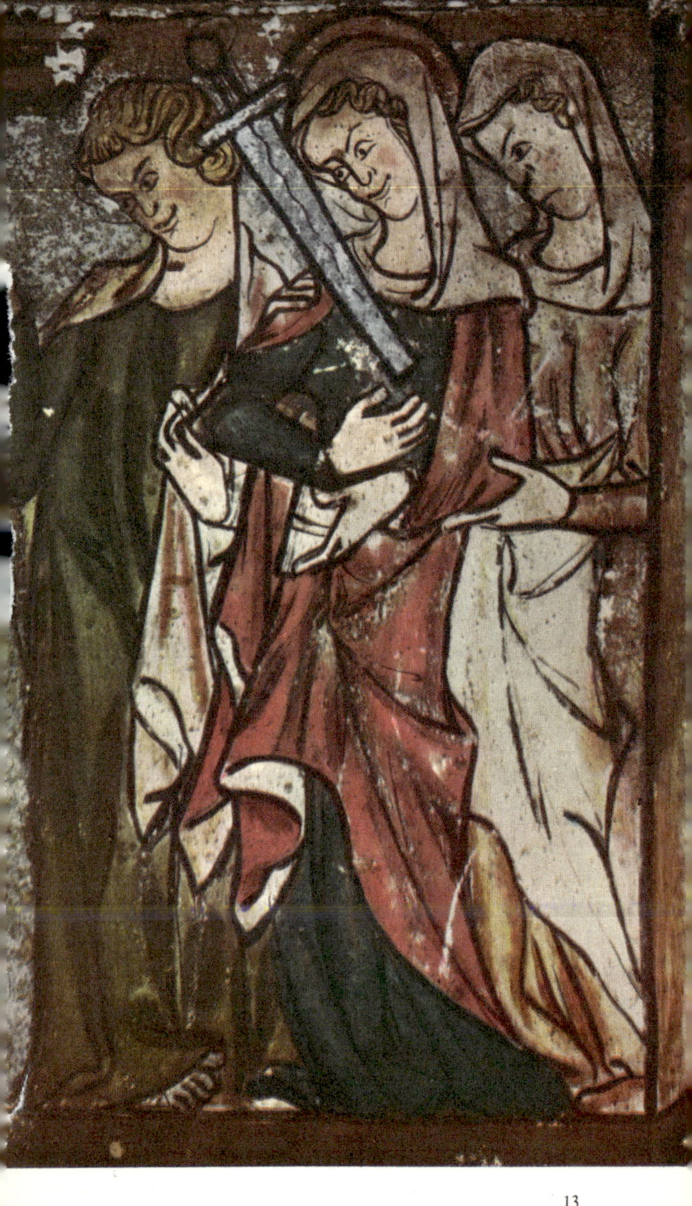

13

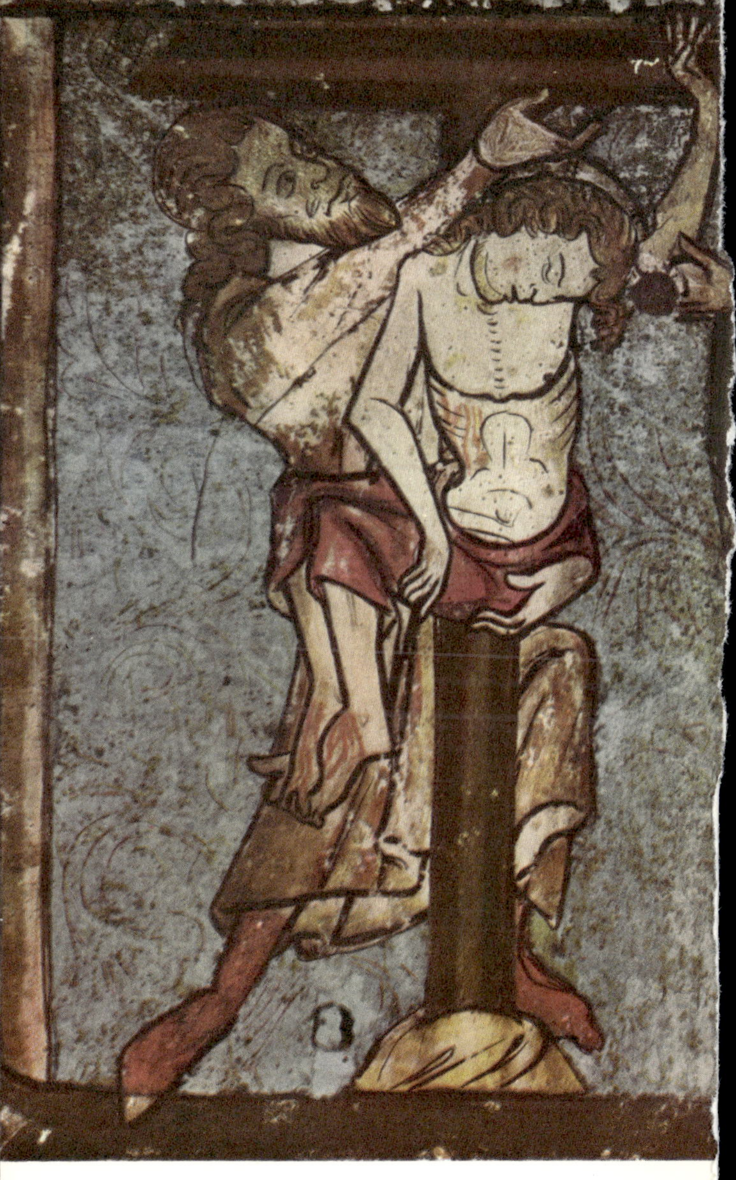

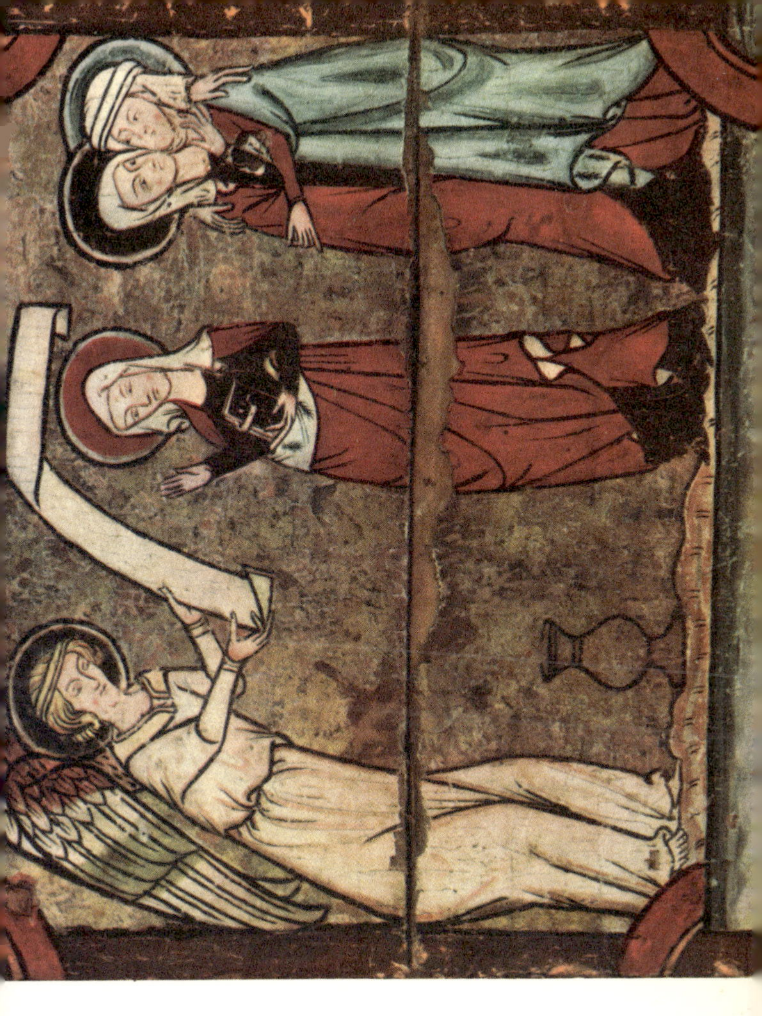

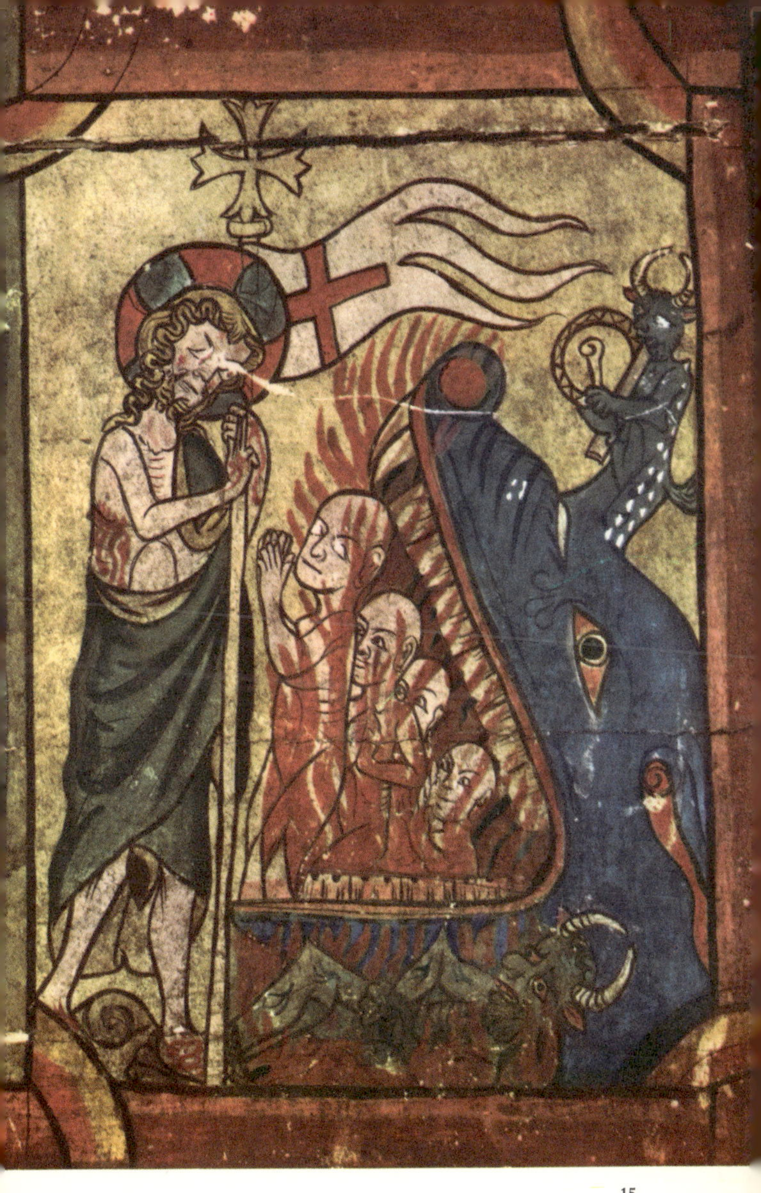

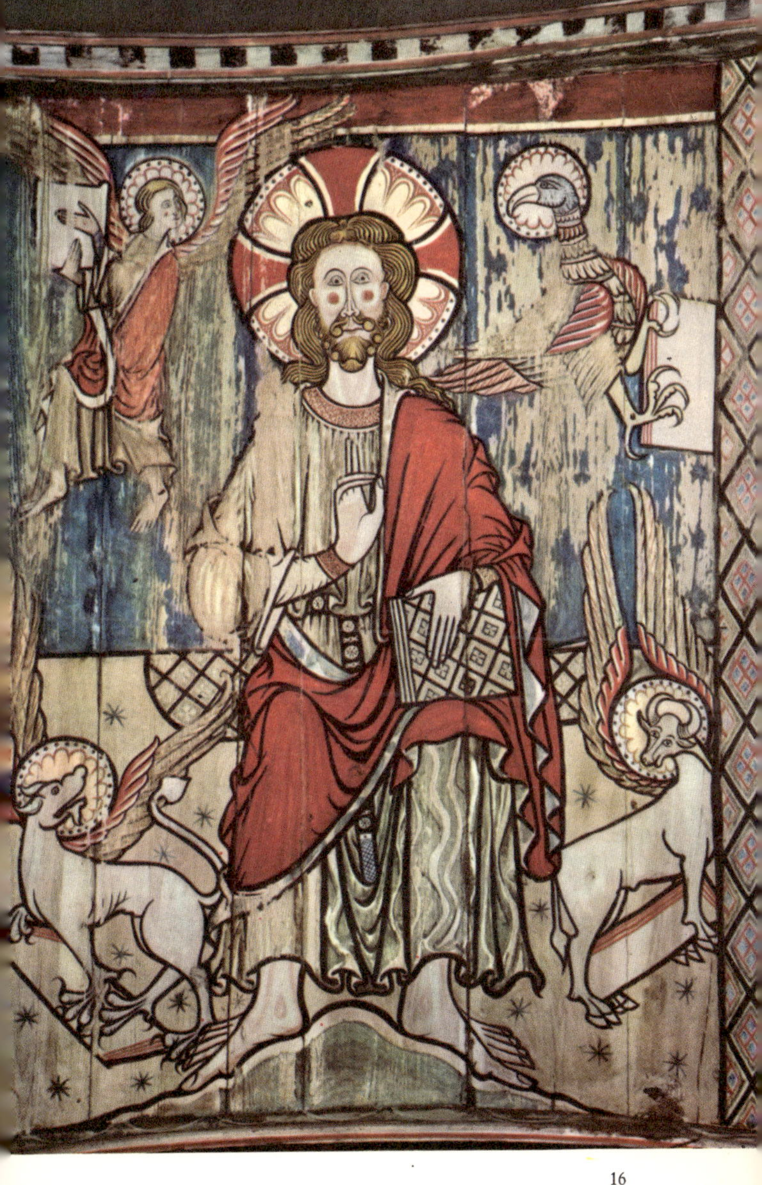

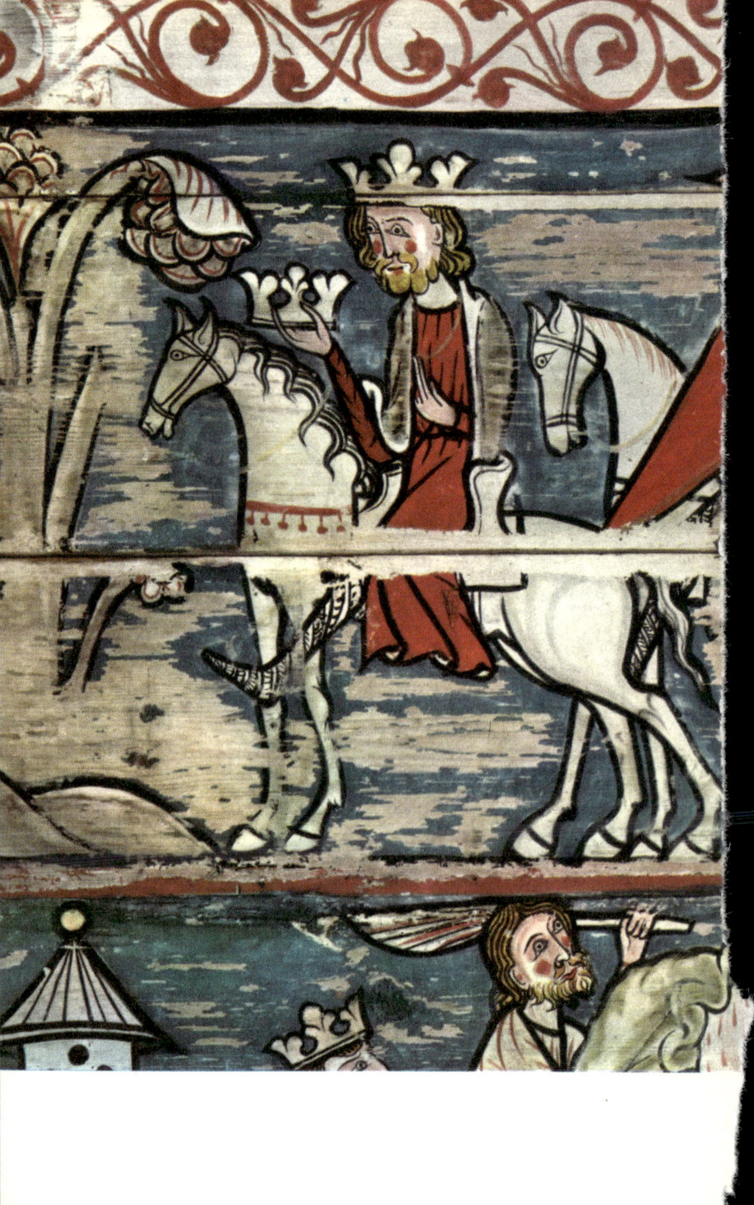

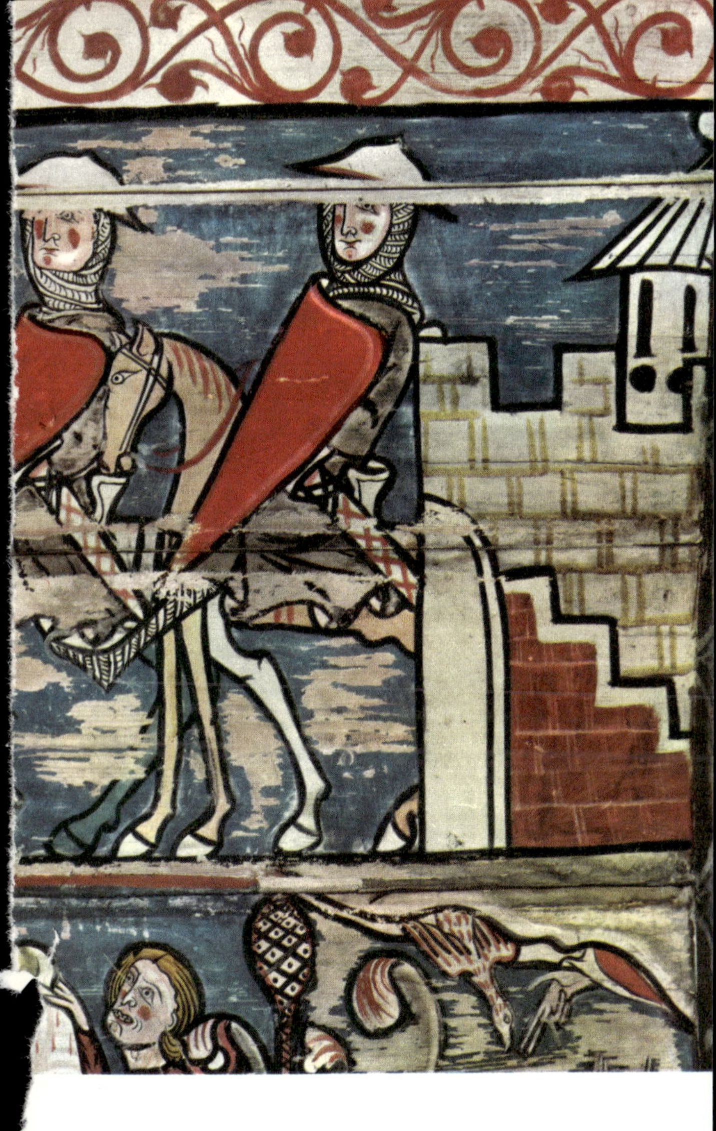

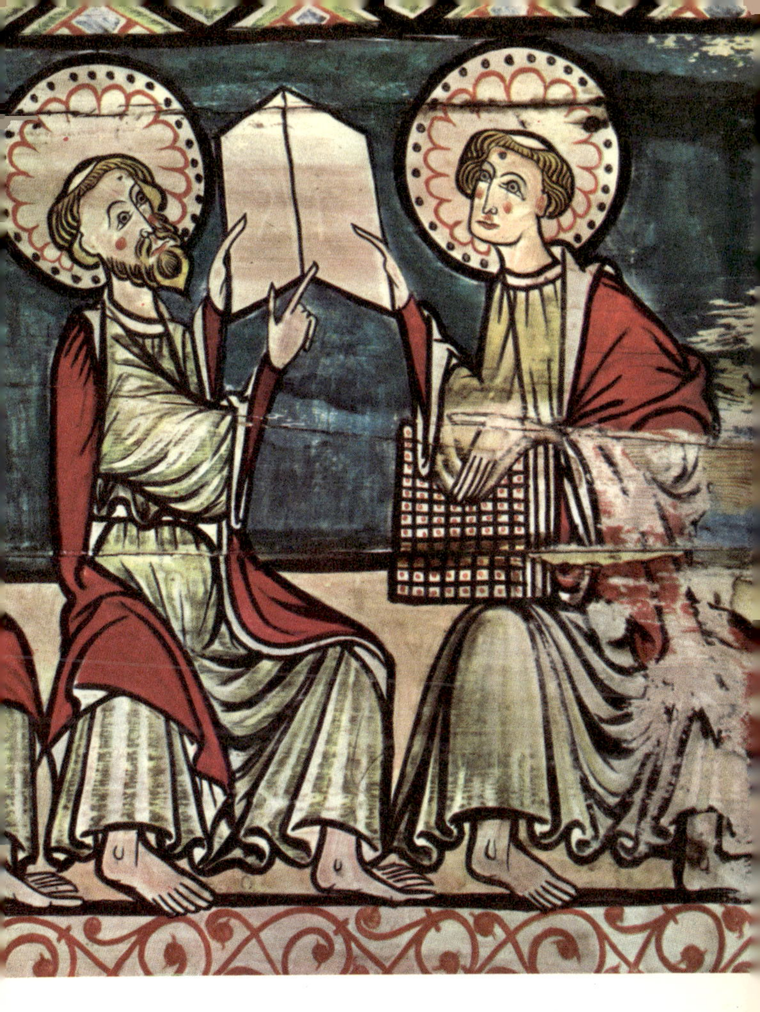

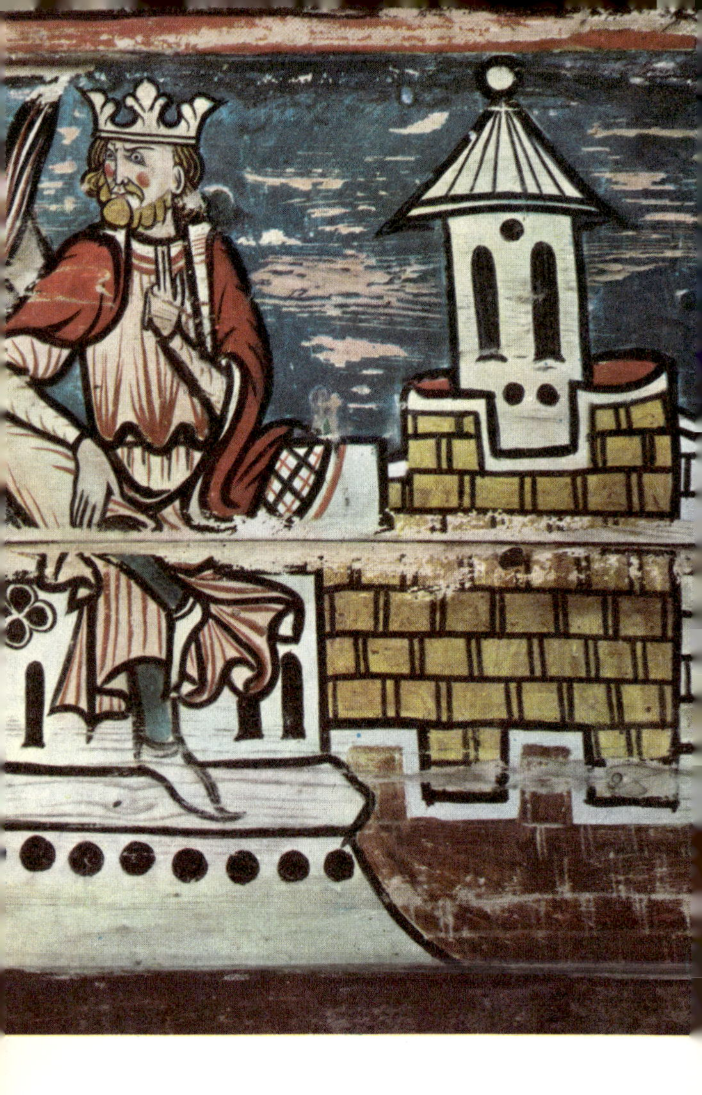

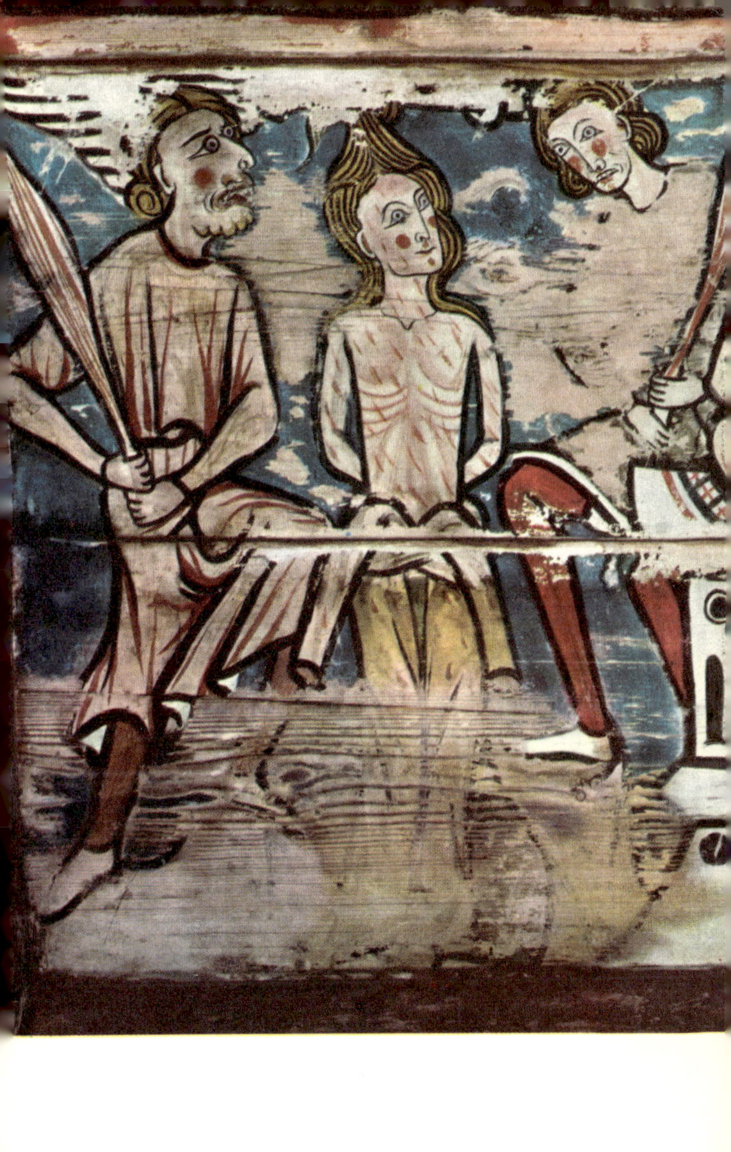

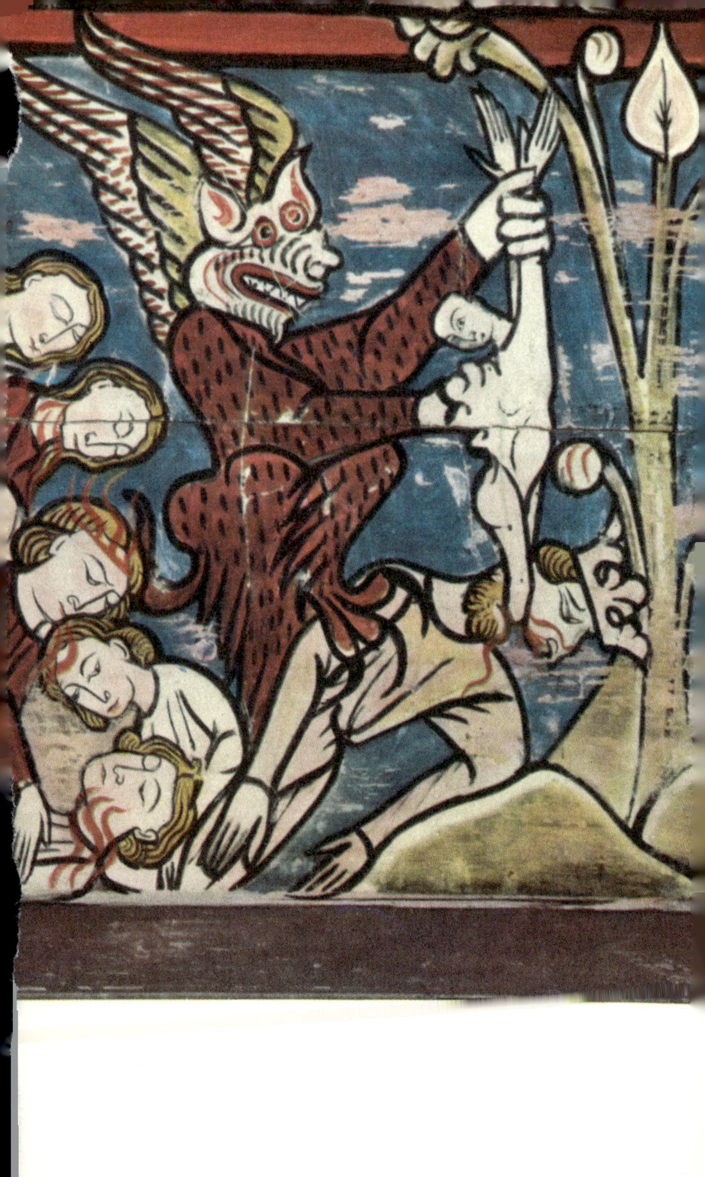

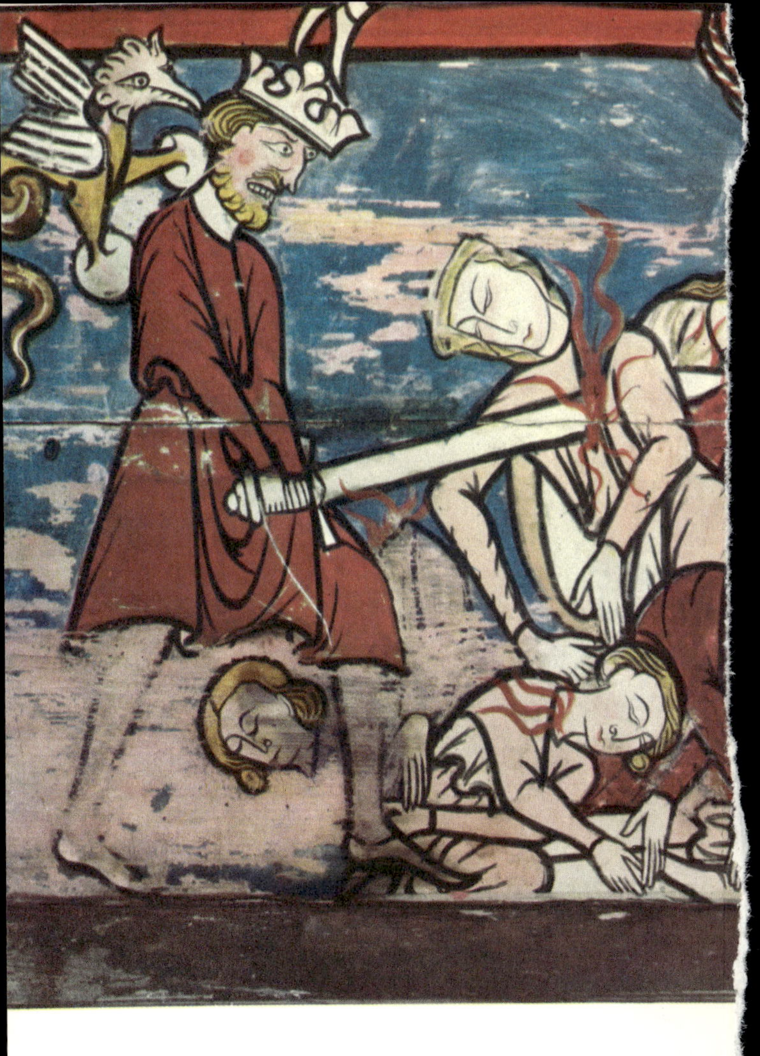

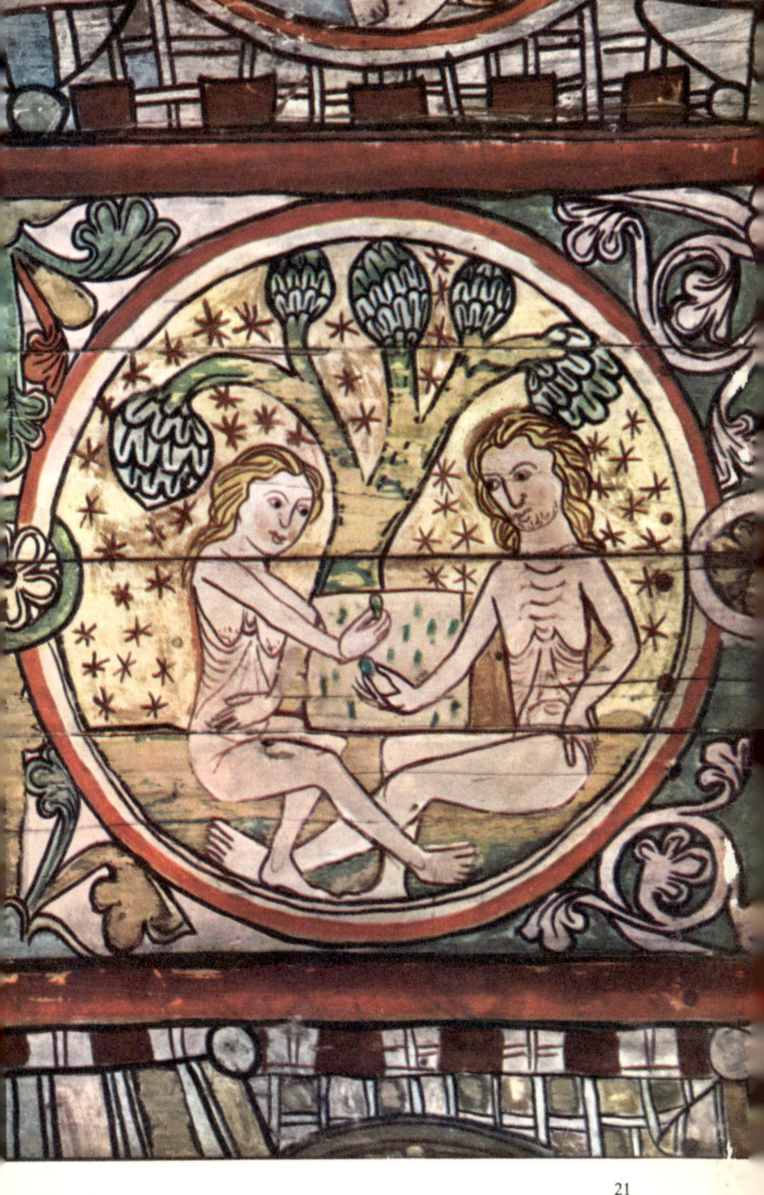

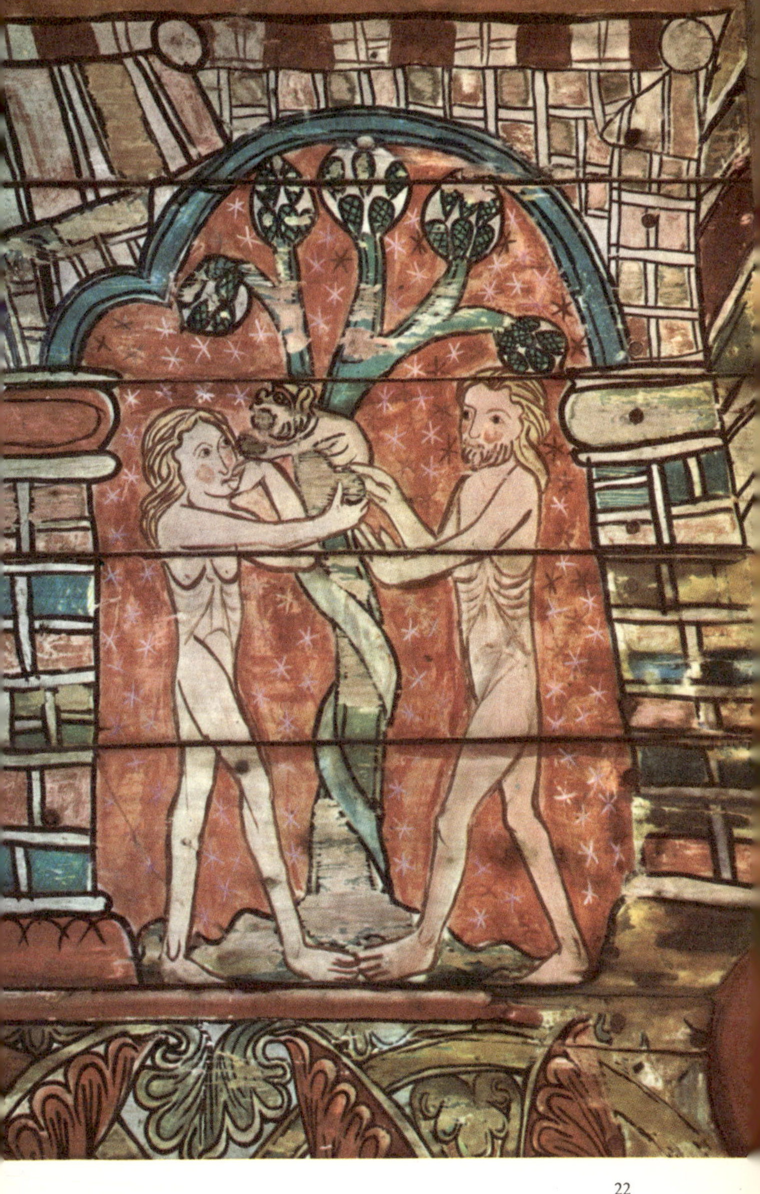

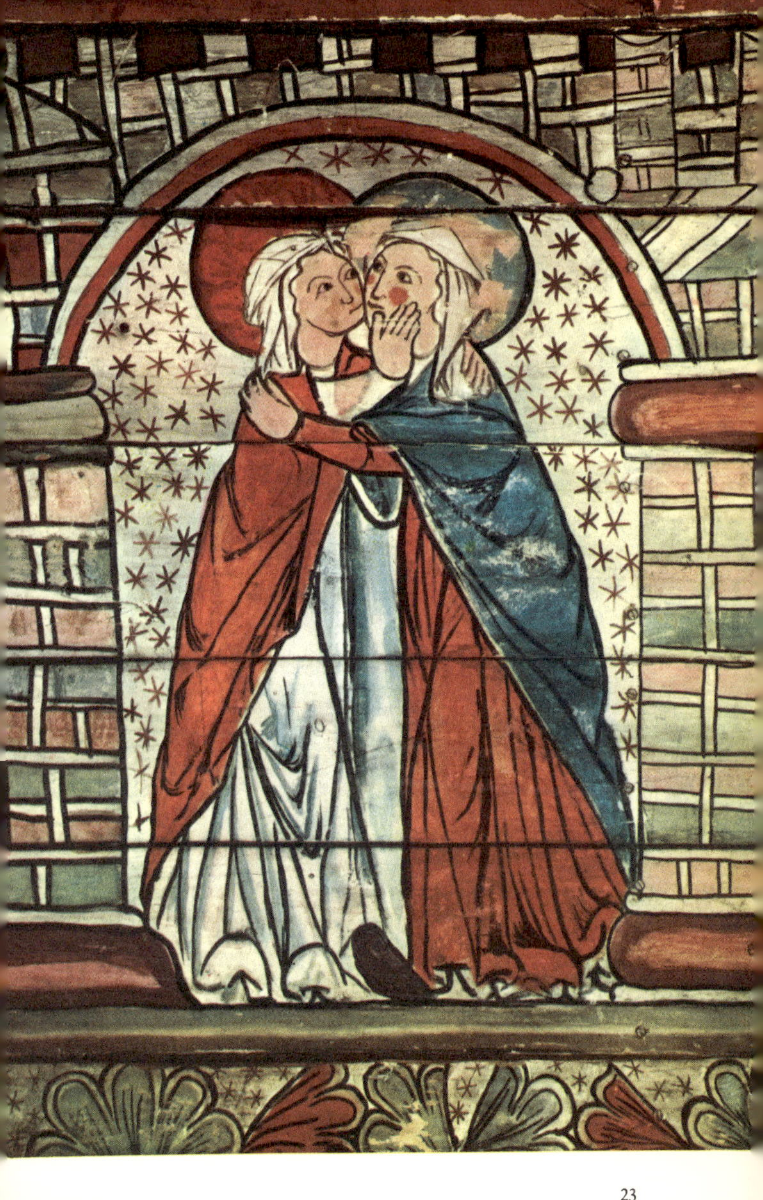

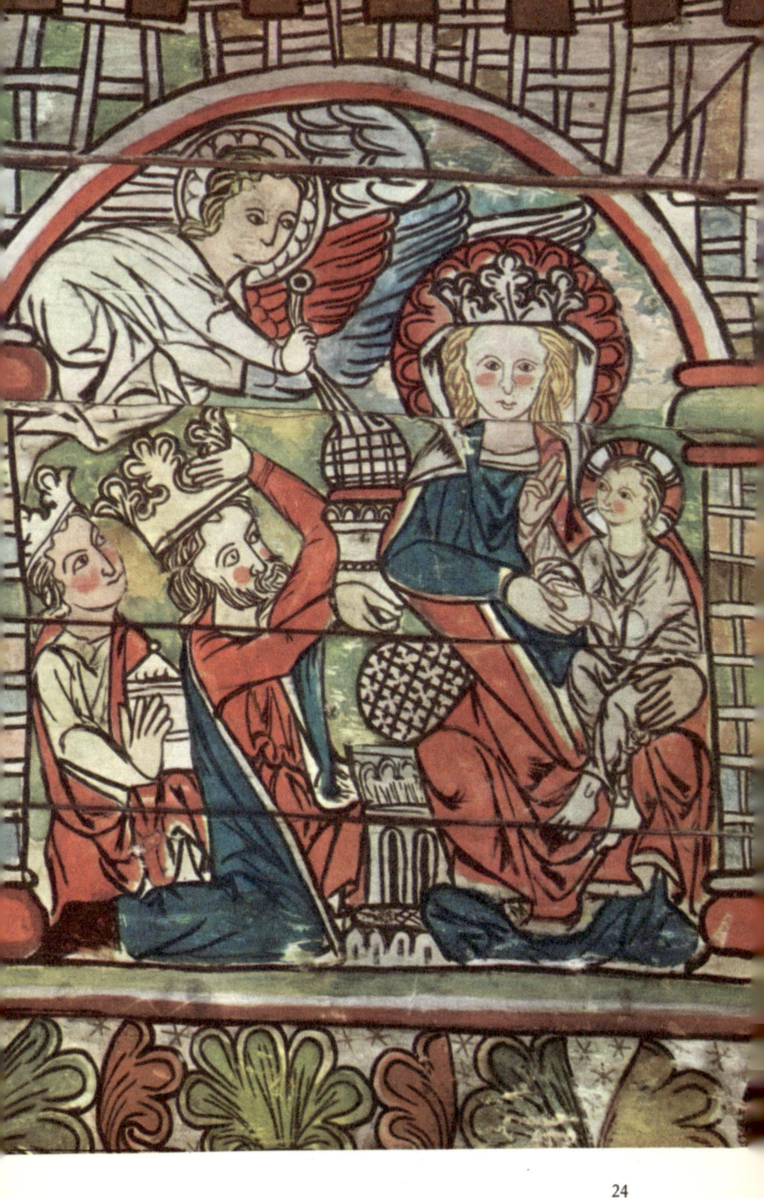

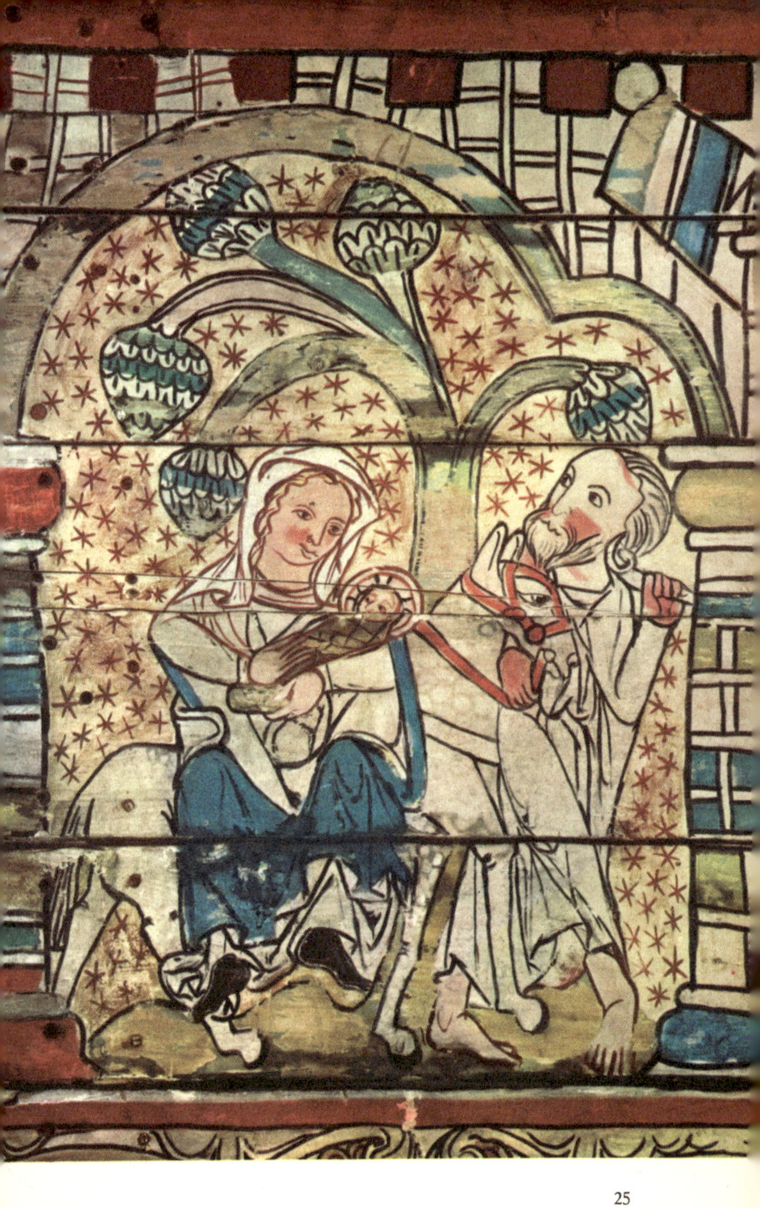

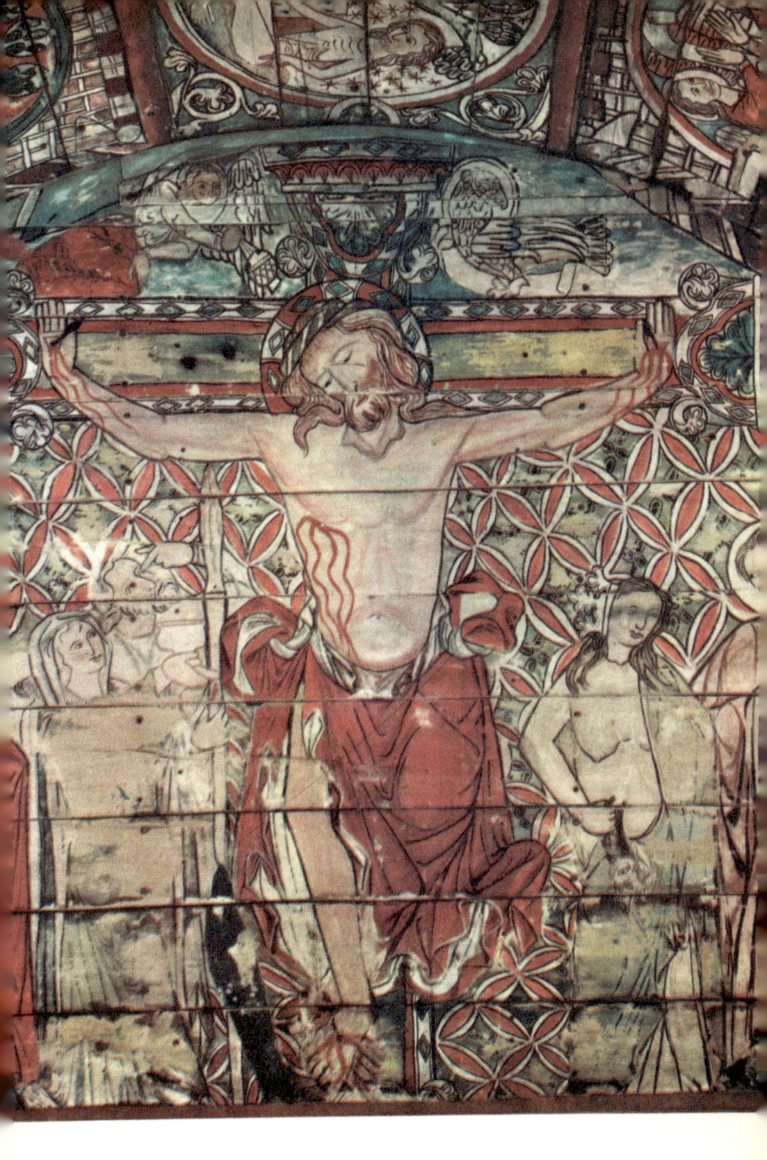

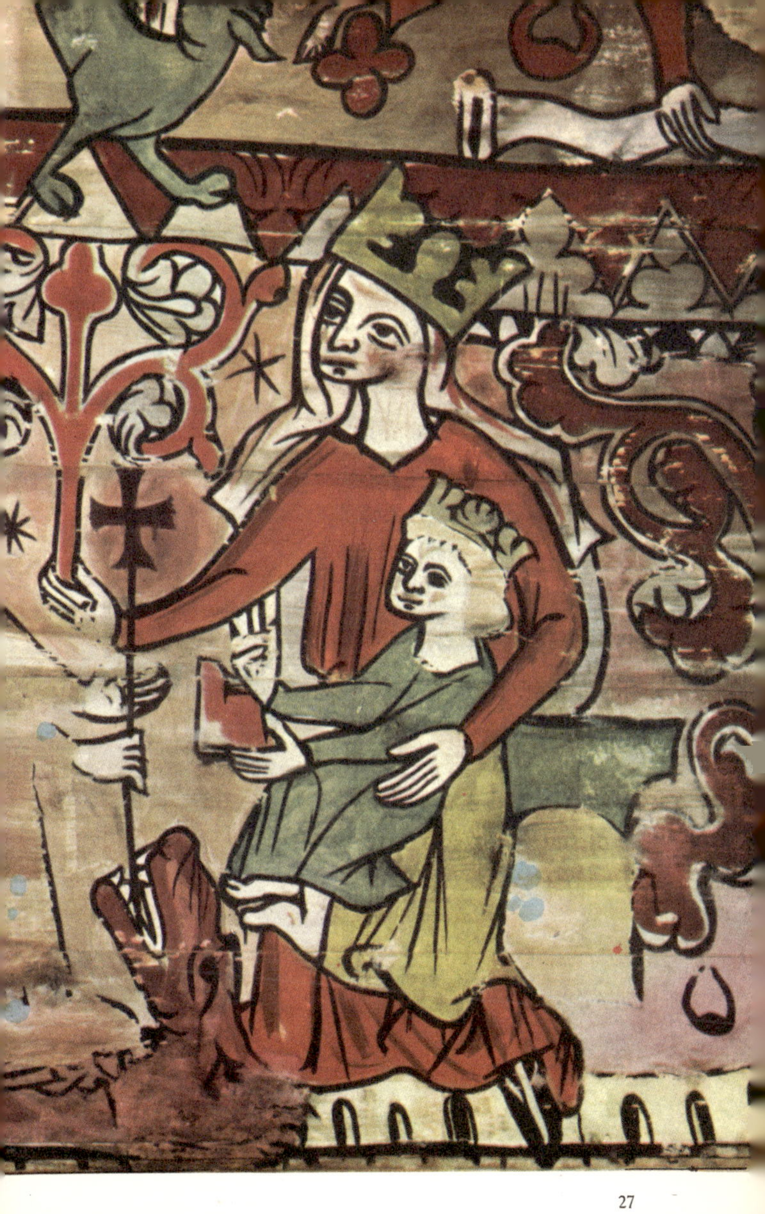

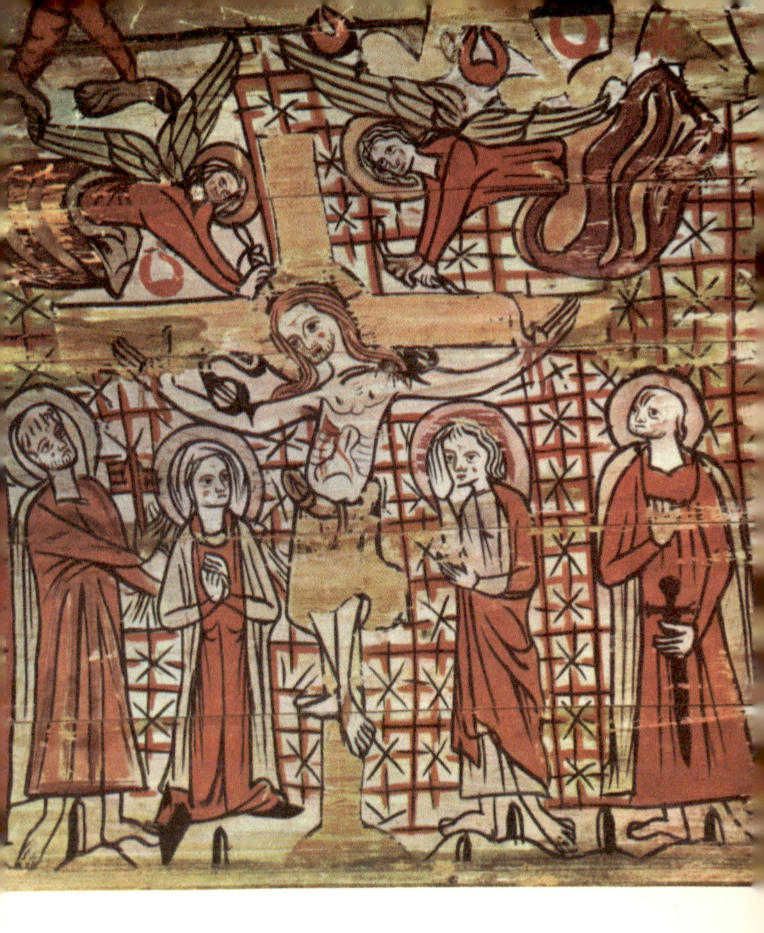

CONTENTS

Continued overleaf ▶

CONTENTS

CONTENTS

The colour photography for the illustrations in this book was carried out by a special Unesco mission which visited Norway for this purpose and to collect the necessary documentation. This mission worked in close conjunction with the governmental authorities of Norway, and Unesco wishes to express its appreciation to all those who collaborated in this work.

BIBLIOGRAPHY

BUGGE, Anders, *Norwegian stave churches*, trans. Ragnar Christopherson, Oslo, Dreyer, 1953, pp. 60-63.

FETT, Harry, *Norges malerkunst i middelalderen*, Kristiana, Cammermeyer, 1917 (in Norwegian, with a summary in French).

LEXOW, Einar, *Norges kunst*, Oslo, 1942, pp. 101-08, 129-40 (in Norwegian).

LINDBLOM, Andreas, *La peinture gothique en Suède et en Norvège*, Stockholm, Wahlström & Widstrand, 1916.

Norway—Paintings from the stave churches, preface by Roar Hauglid, introduction by Louis Grodecki, New York, New York Graphic Society (by arrangement with Unesco), 1955 (Unesco world art series).

ØSTBY, Leif, *Norges kunsthistorie*, revised edition, Oslo, Gyldendal, 1962, pp. 61-63 (in Norwegian).

Printed in Italy